WEIZMANN

HIS LIFE AND TIMES

WEIZMANN

HIS LIFE AND TIMES

H.M. BLUMBERG

ST. MARTIN'S PRESS • NEW YORK

 ROBSON BOOKS • LONDON

First published in 1975 in the United States of América by St. Martin's
Press, Inc., and in the United Kingdom by Robson Books Ltd.

St. Martin's Press Inc., 175 Fifth Avenue, New York, N.Y. 10010
Library of Congress Catalog Number: 75–9465

Robson Books Limited, 28 Poland Street, London W1V 3DB
ISBN 0 903895 34 X

Jacket by Alex Berlyne, Jerusalem
Design by Vivtor Arnon Studios, Tel Aviv
Frontispiece: portrait of Weizmann by Sir Oswald Birley
Printed and bound by Peli Printing Works Ltd., Israel

CONTENTS

ACKNOWLEDGEMENTS

I gratefully acknowledge permission to quote from the following books:

Trial and Error: the autobiography of Chaim Weizmann, copyright by the Weizmann Foundation, reprinted by permission of the publishers, Hamish Hamilton Ltd., of London, and Harper and Row, of New York;

The Impossible Takes Longer: the memoirs of Vera Weizmann, copyright by the Executors of the Estate of the late Vera Weizmann reprinted by permission of the publishers, Hamish Hamilton Ltd., of London;

Chaim Weizmann—Statesman, Scientist, Builder of the Jewish Commonwealth: edited by Meyer W. Weisgal, copyright by Meyer W. Weisgal, reprinted by permission of Dial Press, New York;

Chaim Weizmann: a Biography by Several Hands: edited by Meyer W. Weisgal and Joel Carmichael, copyright by Meyer W. Weisgal and Joel Carmichael, reprinted by permission of Weidenfeld and Nicolson, of London;

Einstein, The Life and Times: by Ronald W. Clark, copyright by Ronald W. Clark, reprinted by permission of the publishers, The World Publishing Company, of New York and Cleveland;

From My Life: the memoirs of Richard Willstätter, translated from the German edition by Lilli S. Horning, copyright by Verlag Chemie Gmb.H., reprinted by permission of the publishers of the English edition, W.A. Benjamin, Inc., of New York;

...So Far: an autobiography by Meyer W. Weisgal, copyright by Meyer W. Weisgal, reprinted by permission of the publishers, Weidenfeld and Nicolson Jerusalem.

I would also like to take this opportunity of acknowledging my gratitude to Mrs Sylvia Flowers, of Rehovot, for her assistance as picture consultant; to Miss Myrna Pollak, of Tel Aviv, Mrs Shulamit Nardi, of Jerusalem, and Mr Julian L. Meltzer, of Rehovot, for helpful editorial suggestions; to Miss Lillie Shultz, of New York, to Dr Anthony Michaelis, of London, and to Mr Ernst Cramer, of Berlin, for locating photographic material; to Mr Shlomo Schwa, of Tel Aviv, for a gift of early picture postcards of Jewish settlement in Palestine; to Mr Shmuel Engelstein and Miss Tamar Deutsch, of the photographic laboratory of the Weizmann Institute of Science, for technical assistance in connection with the photographs; and to Mrs Nellie Hirshfeld, of Rehovot, for her assistance in typing part of the manuscript.

I also wish to thank: the Central Zionist Archives, Jerusalem; the Government Press Information Office, Tel Aviv; the Haganah Museum, Tel Aviv; the Keren Hayesod Archives, Jerusalem; the State Archives, Jerusalem; the Yad Weizmann Archives, Rehovot; the British Information Office, London; and the Mansell Collection, London. I had generous assistance from all of them in compiling the photographic material.

Finally, I would like to acknowledge my debt to my wife, Marion, who encouraged me in this endeavour.

H.M.B.

FOREWORD

A generation which owes so much to Weizmann can in this book see Weizmann the statesman and the scientist, the family man and the friend, against the background of his times. They can discover his own intimate views on events and personalities, can follow in an unfussy record Weizmann's remarkable life story, understand his personality and recognize his hopes and fears, many of them astonishingly relevant and valid today.

Some 30 years ago, in the midst of World War II, I found myself editing a book on Dr. Weizmann. I had gathered round me, as contributors to the volume, a formidable array of distinguished writers and scientists. When the book began to take shape, one of my assistants asked innocently: "Does Dr. Weizmann himself know anything about all this?" I had, in fact, intended the book as a surprise for him, but it then occurred to me that it might indeed be more prudent to tell him about the project before it was finished and I did so in a painstakingly phrased letter. Owing to war conditions, Dr. Weizmann's response was slow in coming, but when it finally arrived, it turned out to be a delicate combination of wit, irony and rebuke. "You might have devoted your energy to some more direct purpose," he chided me, characteristically adding: "If your enterprise is too far gone and beyond recall, please make molehills out of mountains."

During the time that I was somewhat apprehensively waiting for his answer, I read an account of how Winston Churchill had "suddenly emerged from the shadows behind the Speaker's chair in the House of Commons and of the roar of cheering that had gone up there, subsequently echoing throughout the world of the United Nations." In that same account, the question was posed: "What is it that makes a man great?" And the answer, which I cut out and saved over three decades ago is still before me now in a yellowing clipping:

"It is not the infallible correctness of his opinions, for one may sometimes think him wrong and still consider him a great man. It is not consistency, for great men are often great enough to be inconsistent. It is not unvarying success, for great men have their unsuccessful moments. One doesn't know, but somewhere there is a deep mystery of personality. Out of the masses of men, these come when they are needed, out of log cabins and also out of immemorial mansions."

Yes, and also out of the swamps of Motol and the marshes of Pinsk.

Chaim Weizmann and Winston Churchill were born in 1874, only three days apart — Weizmann on November 27, Churchill on November 30. They were two disparate figures born into two totally different environments — one into the aristocracy of enlightened, imperial England, the other into the obscurity of a ghetto village in oppressive, Czarist Russia. One was destined to become a soldier, a writer with rare gifts, an historian with remarkable insights and a Prime Minister of unequalled renown. The other, despite, or perhaps because of his earlier environment, found the ability and the faith to become a highly inventive scientist and a statesman of exceptional historic order, of whom another great British wartime Prime Minister, Lloyd George, had once said:

"...in a thousand years from now his name will be remembered by the Jews, and he will be the only Jew now living whose name will then be remembered"

—a testimony recently endorsed by Lord Boothby, himself an eminent English statesman and parliamentarian:

"Of all the great men I have known, Chaim Weizmann had a kind of greatness I have never encountered in any of the others. He was a prophet, a mystic, a scientist, a philosopher and practical statesman, all mixed up in one compound of inspired clay."

However different they were in upbringing and character, the paths of Churchill and Weizmann crossed early in life and these two leaders formed a life-long friendship and even were in collaboration in World War I, when Weizmann headed the Admiralty laboratory at a time when Churchill was First Lord at Admiralty House.

Now, some fifty years later, in the Centenary year of the birth of these two giants who have changed the course of their peoples' history, two commemorative books of the same pattern have been published — *Churchill, A Photographic Portrait* by the historian Martin Gilbert, and *Weizmann: His Life and Times* by Harold M. Blumberg, of Yad Weizmann. These two books, which I happen to know were prepared without either author knowing what the other was working on, are similar in style and concept. Each in its own way is a postscript to the contemporary, sometimes parallel, sometimes diverging sagas of Churchill and Weizmann.

What Martin Gilbert's *Churchill, A Photographic Portrait* contributes to the massive library of books by and about Churchill, Harold Blumberg's book contributes to the incomparably more slender Weizmann literary legacy. There is Weizmann's autobiography *Trial and Error,* the scholarly editions of *Weizmann's Letters and Papers,* a major project of Yad Weizmann, two books edited by the writer of these lines, *Weizmann — Scientist, Statesman and Builder of the Jewish Commonwealth* (1944) and *Weizmann, A Biography by Several Hands* (1962), and a sundry collection of essays and lectures by historians, publicists and scientists.

I commend the *Weizmann: His Life and Times* as a worthy adjunct of the Weizmann legacy and would like, in addition to my thanks to Mr Harold Blumberg, to express deep gratitude to Mr Barnet Litvinoff, the author, for preparing the biographical essay, as well as to Mr Alex Berlyne of Jerusalem, who designed the book. I wish also to acknowledge the assistance of the Weizmann Archives and its Director, Mr Julian Meltzer, in providing a considerable amount of original source material; and to tender thanks to our partners in this enterprise, the American Israel Publishing Company of Tel Aviv, for their valuable cooperation.

MEYER W. WEISGAL

Rehovot, April, 1975

The Forces That
Shaped Him

Chaim Weizmann as a young boy

The Weizmann home in Motol

Chaim Weizmann was born on 27 November, 1874, the third of fifteen children of Ezer and Rachel-Leah Weizmann, in a wooden house in Motol, a village in the Jewish Pale of Settlement, in Western Russia.

Weizmann had bitter-sweet memories of his birthplace: "Here in Motol, half townlet, half village in one of the darkest, most forlorn corners of the Russian Pale of Settlement, I lived from the time of my birth till the age of eleven; and here I wove my first pictures of the Jewish and Gentile worlds".

Chaim's father was a "*transportierer*... he cut and hauled the timber and got it floated down to Danzig, a complicated and heartbreaking operation," as Weizmann described it, and his mother, Rachel-Leah who married at the age of fifteen was, in her son Chaim's words "...not a good housekeeper... but she was wonderfully good, the kind of person to whom neighbours turn naturally in time of trouble."

Village folk, the Weizmanns of Motol were traditional in their way of life and enlightened in their outlook. The emphasis in their home was always on Zion.

When Chaim was eleven years old, he wrote to his teacher, S.T. Sokolowsky, in passionate terms about "...Jerusalem, which is in our land," ending his letter with a fervent peroration "For why should we look to the kings of Europe for compassion... All have decided: The Jew must die, but England will nevertheless have mercy upon us... — ...to Zion! — Jews — to Zion! let us go!"

Ezer Weizmann was an important person in Motol, the first and only Jew to be appointed *starosta* (head of his village). His children spoke Yiddish at home, learnt Hebrew in the *cheder*, the Jewish school which gave boys, even in a remote village, a high degree of literacy. "Those that wanted to give their children the beginnings of a Russian and modern education engaged a special teacher ...I myself knew hardly a word of Russian till I was eleven years old", Weizmann recalled.

At the age of eleven, Chaim was sent to a school in Pinsk, the large town close to Motol, to a scientific gymnasium. Pinsk shaped Chaim Weizmann's life, as Zionist and as Chemist. By the time he matriculated, seven years later, he had shown an aptitude for Chemistry and a zeal for raising funds for Zionism.

He testified that "...to the one outstanding exception among my teachers, a man by the name of Kornienko, I very possibly owe whatever I have been able to achieve in the way of Science. He was a Chemist, with a genuine love of his subject and a considerable reputation in the world at large... I have often wondered what would have been the course of my life if it had not been for the intervention of this gifted and fine-spirited teacher."

"Our Zionist financial resources were comically primitive. We dealt in *kopeks*," Weizmann recorded. "...I took an active part in these money collections... hour after hour I would go tramping through the mud of Pinsk, from end to end of the town... I worked late into the night, but usually had the immense satisfaction of bringing in more money than anyone else".

Debarred from higher education in Czarist Russia, Jewish students looked westward and flocked to Germany. Chaim Weizmann's choice of Darmstadt Polytechnic for future studies in Chemistry was "...accidental...a friend of the family had a son attending a Jewish boarding-school in the village of Pfungstadt, near Darmstadt ...and I was offered the vacant position of junior teacher of Hebrew and Russian there...I was glad to get out of Pinsk in the autumn of 1892... it was a God-forsaken town...just an enormous rubbish heap".

Pfungstadt's only claim to fame was a brewery. And Weizmann knew Darmstadt only through its desks and laboratories.

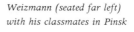

Weizmann (seated far left) with his classmates in Pinsk

The Great Synagogue of Pinsk

In 1894, Weizmann's family moved to Pinsk. "My mother," Weizmann recalled, "was still in Pinsk when the first World War came, and with it, the German invasion. From Pinsk, Mother fled to Warsaw, from Warsaw to Moscow. Already in her sixties, she passed through the storm of the Bolshevik Revolution and the Civil War, came to Palestine in 1921 and lived in Haifa until her death in 1930."

In the same year as Weizmann's family moved to Pinsk, Chaim, then twenty years old, arrived in Berlin to continue his studies. Berlin put Weizmann to the test: whether his Zionism would survive the flood of new ideas in that world metropolis.

"We held our regular Saturday night meetings at a cafe... we never dispersed before the small hours of the morning. We talked of everything, of history, wars, revolutions, the rebuilding of society. But we chiefly talked of the Jewish problem and of Palestine. We sang, we celebrated such Jewish festivals as we did not go home for, we debated with the assimilationists and we made vast plans for the redemption of our people. It was very youthful and naive and jolly and exciting; but it was not without a deeper meaning".

In Berlin, Chaim Weizmann cultivated his life-long love of music:

"Nothing could keep me from Weingartner's Beethoven concerts... we sat in the cheapest seats of course, immediately under the roof. We followed the music passionately and applauded wildly. Toward the close of the Ninth Symphony, we stood up and unable to restrain ourselves, sang along with the orchestra".

When he left Berlin in 1897, Weizmann had completed his work on his doctoral thesis, his belief in the Zionist idea had been strengthened and he was showing an understanding of political strategy. In Berlin, he had formed friendships which would last a lifetime.

Apart from the gaiety and the sparkle which Weizmann remembered from those days, one personality in particular left an unforgettable impression on him, Asher Ginzberg, author and editor (in Hebrew), who had advocated a cultural programme among Jewry as a prior condition for settlement in *Eretz Israel*. Writing under the name of Ahad Ha-am ("One

Of The People''), Ginzberg had settled in Odessa, but for a brief period, which coincided with Chaim Weizmann's few years as a student at the Charlottenburg Polytechnic, Ginzberg was also living in Berlin. ''We youngsters in Berlin did not see much of him'', Weizmann recalled, ''but he was to us, I might say, what Ghandi has been to many Indians, what Mazzini was to young Italy. At rare intervals, we would drop in on him at his modest little home. But his presence in our midst was a constant inspiration...''

Weizmann was enthusiastic about Theodor Herzl's call to Jews to come to the first Zionist Congress, in Basel, in August, 1897. He rallied Zionists from near and far to attend that historic Congress, but by a cruel quirk of fate, was unable to get there himself. ''I had the doleful satisfaction of learning, when I returned to Berlin, that I had been missed at the Congress... my work in the movement was beginning to be known''. Between 1897 and 1950, there were twenty-two Zionist Congresses. Weizmann attended twenty, missing the First, and the Eighteenth Congress (Prague, 1933).

Weizmann went from Berlin to the University of Freiburg, in Switzerland, where he earned a Ph.D., *summa cum laude*, in 1899. His thesis was on chemical reactions in dyestuffs and set him on the road to Geneva, where he was confronted with a crucial choice — application to Chemistry, or dedication to Zionism. It was a dilemma which disturbed him for many years.

QUOD FELIX FAUSTUMQUE SIT

SUMMIS AUSPICIIS

SENATUS POPULIQUE FRIBURGENSIS

EX

DECRETO ORDINIS MATHEMATICORUM ET PHYSICORUM

UNIVERSITATIS FRIBURGENSIS

CUM ERAT RECTOR MAGNIFICUS

OSCARUS VASELLA

HISTORIAE HELVETICAE PROFESSOR ORDINARIUS

QUOS SUMMOS IN REBUS NATURALIBUS HONORES

DOCTORISQUE GRADUM IURA AC PRIVILEGIA

IN

VIRUM DOCTISSIMUM

CHAIM WEIZMANN

DISSERTATIONE SIC INSCRIPTA

Weizmann's Ph.D. degree from University of Freiburg

ÜBER DIE KONDENSATION VON PHENANTHRACHINON UND ξ-ANTHRACHINON MIT EINIGEN PHENOLEN

EXHIBITA

ET EXAMINIBUS RIGOROSIS

IN CHEMIA IN MINERALOGIA NECNON IN PHYSICA

IN HAC IPSA LITTERARUM SEDE MAGNA CUM LAUDE SUPERATIS

ANTE DIEM XXI KALENDAS FEBRUARIAS ANNO MDCCCXXXXVIII

MAURITIUS ARTHUS

ORDINIS MATHEMATICORUM ET PHYSICORUM ILLO TEMPORE DECANUS

CONTULERAT

EOS

POST DIEM XI IUNII

IN EXCELLENTISSIMUM VIRUM QUI

IN EXPLORANDIS NATURAE LEGIBUS SEDO INGENIO CERTAQUE RATIONE DUCTUS

CUM SUMMA IN DOCTRINISQUE ACRIT

TUM MAGNAM IN ARTIS USUM CONVERTIT CURAM

PRAECLARUS PRE MULTIS ANNO TRIBUIT HUIUSCE GENERI BENEDICTA

ISRAELI REI PUBLICAE

FELICITER GERENDAE ADMINISTRANDAEQUE NUNC SUMMA PRAEEST VIRTUTE

DENUO CONTULIT

GRATULANSQUE RENOVAVIT

ALOISIUS MÜLLER

PHYSIOLOGIAE PROFESSOR ORDINARIUS

ORDINIS MATHEMATICORUM ET PHYSICORUM H. T. DECANUS

FRIBURGI HELVETIORUM E DIE XI MENSIS IULII MCMLI

In Geneva, working in Professor Hans Graebe's laboratory and teaching students in the University, he "fought against the dissipation of my energies, the drain on my nervous and physical resources. During those years, we laid the foundations of the Zionist movement among the educated Jewish classes..."

In a letter to a Zionist colleague, Leo Motzkin, in June 1900, he wrote: "There has been so much work of all kinds in the most unrelated fields that I now feel worn out... I have seen the Socialists here unable to utter two words without swearing, spitting or slandering someone three times, and I confess that I am not filled with respect for these representatives of social conscience and social justice. All the Socialism of most of the local people, even of the most outstanding of them, is merely an *Ausfluss* of their own insignificance and individual weakness; they need the crowd to hide behind it, not to educate it ... The general picture is dreadful: *Kein Hirt und eine Heerde*! I myself am very busy with Chemistry..."

Weizmann and Feiwel in Switzerland, 1904

UNIVERSITÉ DE GENÈVE
ÉCOLE DE CHIMIE

LABORATOIRE du Prof. GRAEBE
1902 – 1903

But Weizmann was also very busy with Zionism. He attended the Zionist Congress in London that year. "There was a big meeting yesterday attended by 7000 people." (It was held in the Great Assembly Hall, in the East End of London on 11 August, 1900). And from London, he wrote to a friend in Berlin: "Exhausted and weary, broken morally and physically, I send you greetings, hoping that we may in the near future see at our national assemblies, more life, strength and courage in thought and deed!"

Chaim Weizmann by this time was in love, passionately in love with a young medical student, Vera Khatzman from Rostov-on-the-Don, who was studying in Geneva. He wrote notes to her: "You are bored, and I have a frantic desire to settle down with you in some corner and tell you a lot of things, but there are unwanted eyes. I am not afraid of them, but they profane both of us, or rather — the relationship between us. This gets me down. I am insulted, but I feel better when I look at you, so calm and pure".

The young Vera

When Vera Khatzman went to Clarens for a few days in March, 1901, he wrote to her: "I trust you will be able to protect yourself from intrusion by Russian-Jewish students(?) All that is needed is for someone to come there to deliver a lecture on the immortality of cockchafers and on the influence of Marxism on sojourns in Swiss health resorts, and then arrange a party for the benefit of the Russian idiots... I meant to write you a serious letter, but it has turned out to

Geneva at the turn of the century

Weizmann in his laboratory in Geneva

23

Piccadilly Circus in Edwardian times

be a silly one. It's always like that. However, why not write nonsense? I am fed up with all the brainy, serious propositions such as that two and two make four, or that the whole world is divided into two classes, or that a man's head is the humble servant of a man's stomach or of the stomach of another, stronger man, or that science is a good thing and that it is a pity that the surplus value theory cannot be applied to Darwinism, and so on and so forth. I like gay nonsense. Long live the merry fools, down with the gloomy sages!..." He signed that letter "Your humble slave". And he was!

Their courtship was lengthy and ardent. She was his "Verotchka", "Verunchka", "Verunchik", "Precious Darling", "Sweet Little Girl". He was her "Dear Boy". His heart was full, his mind was active, his life was crowded in those years of his mid-and late-twenties. He was the mainspring of the dynamic Zionist movement among Jewish students not only in Switzerland, but wherever they had congregated to study in the universities of Western Europe. Herzl, an autocrat in conducting Zionist political activity, had to take notice of the chemist who was fast emerging as the spokesman for radical Zionism and the driving force behind the *Judische Hochschule* (Jewish University) project.

"I regard you, Dr. Weizmann, as a person who has been temporarily misled, but nevertheless as a useful force who will once more find his way back and proceed along the tight road together with all of us", Herzl admonished Weizmann, in a patronisingly short reply to a 5000 word letter Weizmann had sent to Dr. Herzl, a few weeks after the Kishinev pogrom in April, 1903. In two days of terror, some fifty Jews were killed, several hundreds were injured and rape and arson took place on a horrible scale. When the grim reports reached him in Geneva, Weizmann wrote to friends in Zurich, "I want to scream and slash out..."

Epitaph to Kishinev — by E. M. Lilien, a contemporary illustrator

He addressed himself to Herzl respectfully but impatiently. "The events in Kishinev have shed a glaring light upon the fate of *one* city. In my travels (Weizmann had visited Russia twice in the recent past, from August to October, 1902, and from March to April, 1903) I made the alarming discovery that distress has grown to a frightening degree... More terrible still is the all-pervading sense of helplessness and perplexity resulting from legal restrictions that grow more severe daily and are to be intensified to a point beyond endurance in the near future. These restrictions are said to be an answer to the growing Jewish revolutionary movement. But the Jewish revolution is the product of unlimited political and economic disabilities. The vicious circle, constantly opening and then closing again, can be broken in both senses only by Zionism... you can form a picture for yourself, dear Doctor, of the kind of environment in which we Zionists labour: in part stubbornly Orthodox, in part petty-bourgeois, and then the assimilating mass, not to mention the proletariat of *Luftmenschen* that defies organisation... in general, Zionism has not so far penetrated to the masses... Zionism must take all measures necessary to strengthen the movement and transfer its centre of gravity outside of Russia. It seems a grave injustice that almost three-quarters of Zionist contributions are made by the neediest Jews — and those who furthermore carry a hundred other burdens — while Western Europe, England and America contribute nothing approaching the proportion demanded by their condition and means... as to the situation in England... you yourself are reported to be far from happy with it... Regarding America, it is best to remain silent... In view of the frightening, catastrophic situation that grows daily more acute, the sphere of West European Zionist activity and responsibility must be greatly expanded ... We must not direct our propaganda effort, as hitherto, exclusively towards the petty bourgeoisie. We must aspire rather to the capture of the intellectuals, and through them of Jewish public opinion as a whole... Jewish culture, being the most vital form of the people's self-expression, is more than a mere part of the national renascence; next to the larger Palestine ideal of Zionism, it represents the only remaining attribute and can at least offer the modern Jew an approach to a loftier view of life..."

The VIth. Zionist Congress, held in Basel in August, 1903, known as "the Uganda Congress", was a turning point in Weizmann's political career. He ceased to pay even lip-service to Herzl's leadership, and diagnosed the considerable support for Herzl's scheme to enlist British aid to settle Jews in East Africa, as "a symptom of a sickness I have warned against for years..." In October, 1903, in a letter to the leading spokesman of the Russian Zionists, and an out-spoken critic of Herzl, Menahem Ussishkin, Weizmann wrote: "The present crisis was inevitable... it is the result

*The only known picture of Weizmann (center right) with
Herzl (center) taken at the Vth Zionist Congress in Basel (1901)*

of the abnormal position of the Jews. One group conceives of
Zionism as a mechanism, and it is ignorant of its connection
with the soul of the Jewish people. Consequently, it seeks
to 'manufacture' Zionism either through diplomatic journeys
or through fund-raising appeals. Elements that are partly
detached from living Judaism — the assimilated Westerners
on the one side, and the Orthodox confined within their
rigid formulae on the other, are incapable of a better understanding of the national cause..."

Weizmann decided to go to England "to find out for
myself, if I could, what there was in the Uganda offer".

On 3 July, 1904, shortly before Weizmann left Geneva to
seek a professional post in London, he learnt of the untimely
death of Herzl. "I feel that a heavy burden has fallen on my
shoulders, and the shoulders are weak and tired", he wrote
to Vera Khatzman, who had become his fiancee and was
visiting her family in Rostov.

The Proving Ground

"I felt that Zionism was at the crossroads... that I too was at the crossroads, and that I had to take a decisive step... a new start had to be made," Weizmann recalled, some forty-five years later, adding "I closed the first chapter of my Zionist life, and set out for England, to begin the second".

It was not in London, however, that he settled, but in Manchester, where he accepted a position as a Demonstrator in Chemistry, at the Victoria University.

In a letter to Vera Khatzman, he confessed: "I used to be concerned exclusively with scholars and students, people untouched by life. I saw the 'real world' only when I was on the road, conducting propaganda, and even then I saw it merely as a pageant. All is changed now. Everything around me is 'real', and so dreary as to be devoid of the faintest poetical haze... materialist, commercial England...".

Slowly, however, he began to pick up the threads of his Zionist activities. In Manchester, he made a bid for recognition by the English Zionists he despised. "Manchester," he recalled with some pride, "became a centre of Zionist thought, which was destined after months and years of laborious effort, to spread out its influence through the surrounding towns and to leave its impress on English Zionism as a whole".

Victoria Station, London (1901)

Victoria University, Manchester,
as Weizmann knew it

In January, 1906, an historic meeting took place between Weizmann and Balfour in Manchester, on the eve of a decisive parliamentary election which Balfour's Tory Party lost to the Liberals, in a landslide, Balfour assessed that transfer of political power in England in these words: "Something more was going on than the ordinary party change... what has occurred here has nothing to do with any of the things we have been squabbling over for the last three years..." Balfour had in mind the transfer of power to a new class, the organised British worker.

Something else had happened, at that memorable encounter between the 'Russian Jewish Chemist', Chaim Weizmann, and Balfour, the languid, urbane Englishman, who said, "I have heard of Dr. Herz" — meaning Herzl — and who questioned Weizmann's insistence that Palestine, and Palestine alone,

"The long line of misery,"
by H.W. Koekkoek: the Russian
retreat in Manchuria

could be the basis for Zionism. "Anything else would be idolatry", Weizmann protested, adding: "Mr. Balfour, supposing I were to offer you Paris instead of London, would you take it?" "But Dr. Weizmann," Balfour retorted, "we have London", to which Weizmann rejoined "That is true, but we had Jerusalem when London was a marsh".

On August 23, 1906, Chaim Weizmann and Vera Khatzman were married.

"Our marriage will take place on the 23rd. of this month at Zoppot, near Danzig, Shefflestr. 10. I cordially invite you, together with our comrades from Odessa, It will make me happy if you were to think of us on that day," was Chaim Weizmann's note of 9 August, 1906 to Menahem Ussishkin in Odessa. In similar vein, he sent invitations to Max Nordau in Paris, Nahum Sokolow in London and to Judah Magnes in New York among his Zionist colleagues.

Having instructed his fiancee which documents to bring from Rostov, he added in his letter to her... "We shall only remain in Zoppot as long as is necessary, and then to Switzerland. The A.C. (Zionist Annual Conference) is fixed for August 27 in Cologne..."

"Concerning these Cologne sessions, I remember chiefly my wife's extraordinary patience and understanding, and my feelings of guilt," Weizmann recalled. "I remember coming home — to the hotel, that is — at five o'clock one morning with a great bouquet of flowers and a basket of peaches as a peace offering".

Wedding day, 19

Weizmann first visited Palestine in 1907, when he took up a challenging invitation from Viennese Zionist and industrialist, Joseph Kremenetzky who had been the first head of the Jewish National Fund on its inception in 1901.

"Dr. Weizmann," Kremenetzky had written in *Die Welt* (official Zionist organ) of 10 November 1906 "is a man of deeds... and complains that he has nothing on which to base effective propaganda for Palestine... Were he to go to Palestine and establish a small chemical industry... I would be willing to assist him".

Thus Weizmann, instead of returning from the Zionist Congress to his wife and six weeks old baby, Benjamin, sailed from Marseilles on the *"Orenoque"* for Jaffa on 22 August, arriving on 10 September. "After a long and unpleassant ordeal... I was obliged to spend five days in quarantine (in Beirut), in a most barbarous Turkish institution... I've told myself several times that I shall never go on such a prolonged trip without you," he wrote to Vera Weizmann.

His next letter to her was in a different tone: "I returned this morning from a tour of the Jewish colonies in Judea, Petach-Tikvah, Rishon-le-Zion, Rehovot. I very much regret not having gone to the colonies directly instead of spending $1\frac{1}{2}$ days in Jaffa, where people concern themselves only with squabbles, gossip and homemade politics, and know only one thing: tearing everything apart. In the colonies, one feels altogether different. It's worth a lifetime to glimpse the work of Jewish hands, to see how after twenty years of toil, former sands and swamps support flourishing orchards, to see Jewish farmers. I understand many things much better, more clearly; the potentiality of Palestine is immense... If everything progresses so slowly, with such difficulties, the fault lies not with the soil of Palestine, nor even with the political conditions in the country — but rather with ourselves — and only ourselves.''

"A dolorous country it was, on the whole, one of the most neglected corners of the miserably neglected Turkish Empire. Its total population was something above six hundred thousand, of which about eighty thousand were Jews, living mostly in the cities, Jerusalem (where they formed a majority of the population), Hebron, Tiberias, Safed, Jaffa and Haifa..." Weizmann recalled many years later. On his return to Manchester, however, he was temperate in his criticism of the regime in Palestine and of the pioneer settlers. A report in the London 'Jewish Chronicle' reported a meeting he had addressed: "He found it difficult to be impartial, for he had gone as 'a lover of Zion'. An opponent could find a hundred reasons to uphold his critical point of view, and a Zionist could find a thousand to show that their hopes not only could be, but were being fulfilled. Palestine was continually changing, improving..."

Jaffa at the time of Weizmann's first visit

ראשון לציון—רחוב במושבה
Rishon-le-Zion — A street at the Colony

Early postcard pictures of
Jewish settlements in Palestine

רחובות
Rehoboth

גדרה
Gedera

In 1909, Vera undertook a long and arduous journey to
Russia with their infant son, to visit their families in Rostov
and Pinsk. Chaim, lonely and dejected, wrote to her: "It is
already an eternity — or so it seems to me — since you went
away with the little one and left the house empty... loneliness
in Manchester seems twice as pronounced, twice as deep and
there is no one to soften the roughness of local life. Sometimes
I have a strong wish to go away for good, to some place where
one would not have to sell one's soul, one's brains, for a mess
of pottage".

That letter was followed a few days later with another, in
which he announced: "I received an offer of a post (Professorship) in India (Calcutta)... I have, of course, refused it."

His dissatisfaction was due not only to frustration and
impatience about his career, but also to his feeling of aliena-
tion. A few months after he had turned down the offer to go
to India, he wrote to a Zionist colleague in Jaffa: "You are
close to the cause, whereas I, with all the glitter of a well-
made career, would immediately swop this career for a
modest abode at the foothills of the Judean hills... You want
to come to England? Let me tell you that England is a difficult
country..."

When David Wolffsohn, President of the World Zionist Organisation in succession to Herzl, visited London in 1910, Weizmann denied charges that he had been leading an intrigue against the President. "It was never my intention to lead the Movement," he remonstrated, "My purpose was to prepare myself for Palestine".

The Weizmanns of 57 Birchfields Road, Rusholme in Manchester were by now, however, typically 'English suburban', and while Chaim was dividing his time between his academic obligations and laboratory work and his Zionist political activities which took him up to London and sometimes across to the Continent, Vera was struggling to keep their home going on his income of £350 a year, of which £50 was allocated for buying the books Chaim needed. She decided she would sit for the English medical degree. "But who will look after us?" was Chaim's first reaction, as Vera remembered it — and her retort: "For a change you'll have to look after yourself!"

That was in 1911. She did not take her finals before two more years of study, struggle and sickness.

57, Birchfield Road, Rusholme
Dr. Weizmann's first own home in Manchester.
The building on the left, No 55, is the house of Mrs Dreyfus, the widow of Dr. Charles Dreyfus, founder of Clayton — Aniline, Chairman of the Manchester Zionist Association, and the man who introduced Weizmann to Balfour in 1906

Vera Weizmann (extreme right) at a garden party in Manchester

Faculty members, and families, Owens College

In the Zionist world, however, Chaim's fortunes were changing. The Xth. Zionist Congress of 1911 brought about Wolffsohn's demission from the Presidency, and Weizmann was brought into the inner circles of Zionist policy-making, by the new regime which now had its headquarters in Berlin.

From the unlikely base of Manchester, he planned and implemented a long-term attack on a project which he had begun in Geneva and which he would see through to its ultimate sucess in Jerusalem — the establishment of a Jewish University.

He had few illusions about the condition and future of Jews in Central and Eastern Europe. In 1911, he observed to Vera, in a letter from Warsaw: "Jewish life here is a *totentanz*, a *danse macabre*... ostentatious over-dressing, over-flowing cafes, gaiety and amusement, while the screw turns tighter and tighter, the circle of misfortune gets narrower".

A Family Portrait —
Ezer and Rachel Weizmann
surrounded by their children

He summed up his status in a letter to the Zionist leadership in Berlin, at the end of 1911: "My connections extend mainly to the academic world here. I know Balfour, to whom I talked about Zionism some years ago. I know Haldane, the brother of the present War Secretary, I know Lord Morley, who is rector of our University... if I had something positive to tell people, it would not be too difficult to approach them and they would give me a ready hearing... the only way for us to approach the English is to show them how vital it can be for England to have a friendly and 'strong' element in Palestine... we can be the link between England and the Muslim world".

Among his close friends in Manchester were Professor Arthur Schuster, a prominent scientist, and his wife, Caroline and daughter, Nora; Charles Dreyfus, industrialist and Zionist and his wife, Ada; and, by 1913, Rebecca and Israel Sieff and Miriam and Simon Marks; and a lawyer, Harry Sacher, who was also a journalist on the staff of the *"Manchester Guardian"*.

His methodical, intensive and visionary campaign for the Jewish University brought him into contact with men of high reputation; Paul Ehrlich, of Frankfurt-am-Main, Nobel Prize laureate for his work on immunology (1908); Baron Edmond de Rothschild and his son, James, of Paris; Dr. Judah Leib Magnes, Rabbi of Temple Emanu-El of New York. It also brought him into opposition with those who wished to accelerate the pace of the establishment of the University.

Weizmann was adamant that the standards of the University were to measure up to the Pasteur Institute in Paris and Ehrlich's Institute in Frankfurt, in the sciences; and to be unrivalled in Jewish Studies and in the humanities.

One who was particularly impatient was the Russian Zionist, Vladimir Jabotinsky, whose views were mocked at by Weizmann in a letter to the Zionist Executive in Berlin: "They want a teaching institute straight away, because an urgency exists in Russia... we fought against the Utopia of the Charter and educated the Party to view Zionism as a historic evolution. Now, in the realisation of the *greatest* national project, these same fighters again want to tread the ground of belief in miracles, of Zionism living by the grace of antisemitism. ...we can say straight away that we are already awarding diplomas... the future 'professors' can be dragged around the whole Diaspora in cages and collect money, but this won't make it a University, only a monstrous blot... If the gentlemen believe they can conjure books, a language of instruction, professors, money, science, out of the ground, let them find bliss in their belief."

As research chemist and lecturer, Manchester

Weizmann himself was hoping to do research work and to teach in Palestine, at the existing higher educational institution, the *Technikum* in Haifa. "...when I get the Chair of Biochemistry in the *Technikum*", he wrote to Ahad Ha'am, early in 1912, and a few weeks later he confided to a Zionist colleague in Berlin, "As you know, I want to go to Palestine in three to four years. But I want to go to Palestine not when I have nothing to lose here, but on the contrary, after having achieved everything here".

Apart from domestic crises, and the disappointment of being overlooked for a Professorship at the Victoria University, the years immediately preceding the First World War were years of constructive work for Weizmann. He was respected among his academic and Zionist colleagues. He was working to a plan, for Zion and for himself.

His "lab" in Owens College

Chaim, Vera and their firstborn, Benjie

Then the war broke out, on 4 August, 1914.

The Weizmanns were marooned in the Rhone Valley, at the start of a holiday in Switzerland, when Britain declared war on Germany.

There had been premonitions. "It's strange to remember", Weizmann wrote, thirty-five years and two world wars later, "how these premonitions of ours never crystallized into an actual belief. Yes, there would be a war somewhere, sometime; war was inevitable, but it had nothing to do with the here and now."

On July 28, 1914, Weizmann wrote to a close Zionist colleague in Berlin, Yehiel Tschlenow: "...What will happen to all our work, if war really does break out, God knows. I cannot even imagine it. It is such a fearful catastrophe..."

Six weeks later, in a letter to Shmarya Levin, a close associate of his since early Congresses, then in New York, Weizmann reported: "In Europe, as you can well imagine, everything has come to a standstill; only the roar of the guns can be heard." In the same letter, Weizmann reported a meeting he had had in Paris with Baron Edmond de Rothschild, whose opinion was that: "Although things look black... we could win the war. The war would spread to the Middle East and there things of great significance to us would happen".

In the first weeks after the outbreak of the war, Weizmann was already taking steps to precipitate some of those "things of great significance". He arranged to meet C.P. Scott, the influential Editor of the 'Manchester Guardian' — a man whom Weizmann described in a letter after that meeting "... carries great weight and expressed his willingness to see Grey (then British Foreign Secretary) when we have a proposal to submit".

Scott arranged for Weizmann to meet Lloyd George, then Minister of Munitions, Winston Churchill, then First Lord of the Admiralty and Herbert Samuel, one of the leading members of the Liberal Party, and the first professing Jew to have been a member of a British Government.

"Will it be possible to raise a Jewish voice also, when there is talk of peace, when the interests of small nations are to be safeguarded? "Weizmann asked Shmarya Levin, in a letter towards the close of 1914.

*Photo on his first
British passport issued in 1915*

Baron Edmond de Rothschild,
flanked by his bodyguard
Avraham Shapiro,
on a visit to Palestine

The "Jewish voice", that of Chaim Weizmann, would be raised at the right time and in the right places, to safeguard Jewish interests. But first, he was concerned about achieving Jewish unity.

He appealed to Israel Zangwill, the noted Anglo-Jewish author, who had been a resolute supporter of Herzl's 'Uganda Scheme' and was the founder of the anti-Zionist "Territorialist" Movement: "Whatever differences of opinion have separated you from the general Zionist body, differences which I am afraid are still in existence, I am nevertheless convinced that at the present critical moment, we must try... working together... and save what can be saved from this debacle which befell our people".

The "Jewish Voice"

Israel Zangwill

From the outset of the war, Weizmann's avowed intent was to get from the British Government, a firm commitment to a National Home for the Jewish people after the war. He associated himself, from the early days of the war, with another Jewish national cause — the formation of a Jewish fighting force, an idea originally conceived by two Russian Jews independently of each other. One was Weizmann's Zionist colleague, Vladimir Jabotinsky, the other was Pinkas Ruttenberg, then living in exile in Italy, a man who would return for a short time to play an important part in Kerensky's short-lived democratic Russian Government, but would eventually be identified with Palestine.

Although Weizmann was only lukewarm at first to Jabotinsky's scheme for a Jewish force to fight alongside the Allies against the Central Powers, he lent his support to Jabotinsky's campaign, to the extent that Jabotinsky himself was moved to write, in an article in a Copenhagen Zionist newspaper, in October 1915: "Almost nothing is being done ...and if it is still 'almost', it is the personal merit of one man in Manchester. It was his merit that the ground was prepared in certain influential English circles. If it were not for him (Weizmann), we would have had in England the same situation we now have in other countries of the Entente: nothing!"

By 1915, Weizmann was working for the British Admiralty. His invention of a process to produce acetone by fermenting maize proved to be a signal contribution to the British war effort, enabling England to maintain vital supplies of gunpowder, at a time when the Germans were poised to blockade the British Isles, and the ubiquitous "U"-boats were raiding successfully in the Atlantic Ocean.

When he began his work for the Admiralty, Winston Churchill was First Lord at Admiralty House and Lloyd George was Minister of Munitions. For a short time, Balfour

Sergeant Vladimir Jabotinsky of H. M. Armed Forces

Benjamin Weizmann

succeeded Churchill at Admiralty House, and Weizmann had access to these three men, through his work as a scientist and his connections with C.P. Scott.

At first, Weizmann travelled backwards and forwards by train between Manchester and London, until, in Vera's words, "worn out by the constant travelling, he took a small apartment in Chelsea, which he shared for a while with Vladimir Jabotinsky. I continued my medical work in Manchester since a replacement could not be easily found in wartime. But early in 1916, I came to live in London. We set up home first in Campden Hill Road and a year later at 67 Addison Road" (The Weizmanns lived there for four years, until they bought a house in Addison Crescent, Kensington, which remained their London address for twenty years).

In his single-minded determination to achieve the Zionist objective of a National Home, Weizmann enlisted the support of many notable Gentiles, but he and his fellow-Zionists had to contend with bitter opposition from within the ranks of Anglo-Jewry, particularly from their acknowledged leaders.

Edwin Montagu, at one time Financial Secretary to the Treasury, and in Lloyd George's Government, Secretary of State for India, was one of them. Although staunchly upholding Jewish tradition and civic rights, he was an uncompromising opponent of Zionism. Weizmann was to recall, at a later stage, the assessment of Montagu by Balfour's niece, Blanche Dugdale: "Edwin Montagu could not extend to his own people the sympathy he evinced later for the national and religious rights of the Indians and Muslims".

Thanks to Weizmann's efforts and skilful diplomacy, the Zionist cause was making considerable political headway in England. At the same time, it was receiving increasing recognition elsewhere.

In April, 1917, Weizmann wrote to Harry Sacher, who from 1915–1919 was a member of the editorial board of the "Manchester Guardian", "As you know, public opinion and official circles in France know very little of Zionism... in the opinion of Sokolow and also of Baron Edmond (de Rothschild) ...they have succeeded in impressing the French with the importance and value of our movement... the French agreed to all Jewish national claims as expressed in our Demands, without, reference, of course, as to who is going to be the suzerain power in Palestine".

Albert Thomas, Edwin Montagu and Lloyd George, Minister of Munitions (1916)

Weizmann explained: "What we did not know in the early stages of our practical negotiations was that a secret tentative agreement, which was later revealed as the 'Sykes-Picot Treaty', already existed between France and England", regarding the future of the Ottoman Empire's colonies in the Middle East.

A telegram Weizmann sent to Mr. Justice Louis D. Brandeis, counsellor to President Wilson and the first Jew to be appointed to the U.S. Supreme Court, in April, 1917 testifies to the supremacy of Brandeis in the Zionist movement in the U.S., and of Weizmann in effective Zionist leadership: "After careful consideration between all leading Zionists and friends like Ahad Ha'am, Rothschilds and Herbert Samuel and discussion with competent authorities unanimous opinion only satisfactory solution Jewish Palestine under British Protectorate."

Following on the abolition of all restrictions on Jews in Russia, by the Provisional Government after the February Revolution of 1917, Russian Zionists held a Conference in June. Weizmann, Norman Bentwich and Joseph Cowen sent a telegram to Rosov, leader of the Russian Zionists "Heartily congratulate the Zionists of Free Russia assembled to deliberate

upon national freedom of our people. May you steadily keep in view unity of our nation and permanency of the settlement to be attained. We must work for... an autonomous Jewish Palestine for the Jewish Nation". That was the last Zionist Conference to be held in Russia.

Weizmann had no illusions about the thaw in the Russian political situation. Writing to C.P. Scott, on 13 September, on the eve of the Bolshevik Revolution, he said: "I quite understand that everybody is preoccupied now with the grave situation in Russia... I am afraid that even if Kerensky suceeds now in establishing a semblance of order, it will only be of a very short duration... the elements constituting the Soviets are not constructive, they are narrow-minded and fanatical. The misfortune of Russia is that it possesses a small group of intellectuals inexperienced in statecraft and a huge mass of inert peasants who can be swayed by political demagogues... the peasants are told by the Soviets that they are called upon to establish a millennium in Russia..."

A letter from Weizmann to Sir Ronald Graham, Assistant to the British Foreign Secretary (13, June, 1917) reveals the extent of worldwide Jewish support for Zionist claims, and highlights a new trend in the attitude to Zionism, inhibited since 1914 by Germany's alliance with the Turks: "There is little doubt that the German Government would view favourably attempts made by the Zionists of the world in favour of peace propaganda... it is noteworthy that only about two or three months ago, the German press wrote comparatively little about the Zionist Movement, although there is a very powerful Zionist Organisation in Germany and Austria, which has increased in strength and vitality still more since the occupation of Poland and Lithuania, but lately articles of an extraordinary character have begun to appear in the German Press which deal with the great importance of the Zionist Movement, and the great danger which a Jewish Palestine would represent to the Central Powers. Such articles appeared chiefly in the conservative, semi-official German Press and also in some of the more liberal papers like the *Frankfurter Zeitung*. Another interesting fact in connection with this is the attitude of the *Neue Freie Presse*. This paper had for a long time as one of its Editors Dr. Herzl, the founder of the Zionist Movement, but it never wrote a single line about Zionism in its columns. It recently opened its columns not only to Zionist articles, but it publishes regularly the subscriptions to Zionist funds like the Jewish National Fund. There can be no doubt about it, that a change of front has taken place and orders have been given to treat Zionism as an important political factor in policy in Central Europe... a policy calculated to influence Jewish public opinion in America and Russia... more than half of the Jewish population of Russia has declared for Zionism. In America, an all-Jewish Convention is going to take place soon, the elections of delegates have

Sir Herbert Samuel and Baron Edmond de Rothschild

already been effected and the majority elected is Zionist. The United Italian Jewish Community not only support our Palestine aspirations but would support a British Protectorate. The South African Jewish Community and Canadian Jews have expressed approval of Zionist policy..."

The intensive round of meetings and missions, which had begun in February, 1917, with a conference between representatives of the British Government and leading Zionists, had continued with representations by Weizmann's Zionist colleague, Nahum Sokolov to the French and Italian Governments and to the Vatican, and with discussions between Weizmann, Lloyd George, Balfour and other members of the War Cabinet, including the South African, General Smuts, reached its climax when in October, 1917, President Wilson gave unequivocal support to the principle of recognising Palestine as the National Home of the Jewish People.

The decisive meeting of the British Cabinet took place on 31, October. Weizmann was waiting outside in a Whitehall passage. The Cabinet approved a text which had been prepared by Leopold Amery. He and Mark Sykes were the two Political Secretaries to the War Cabinet. When Sykes brought out the document, which the Cabinet had authorised Balfour to publish in the form of an official letter to Lord Walter Rothschild, he exclaimed: "Dr. Weizmann, it's a boy!"

The Balfour Declaration, at right

Balfour and Smuts leaving an Imperial War Cabinet meeting

Foreign Office,

November 2nd, 1917.

Dear Lord Rothschild,

I have much pleasure in conveying to you, on
behalf of His Majesty's Government, the following
declaration of sympathy with Jewish Zionist aspirations
which has been submitted to, and approved by, the Cabinet

"His Majesty's Government view with favour the
establishment in Palestine of a national home for the
Jewish people, and will use their best endeavours to
facilitate the achievement of this object, it being
clearly understood that nothing shall be done which
may prejudice the civil and religious rights of
existing non-Jewish communities in Palestine, or the
rights and political status enjoyed by Jews in any
other country".

I should be grateful if you would bring this
declaration to the knowledge of the Zionist Federation.

Yours

Arthur James Balfour

Lord Rothschild on his estate at Tring, Hertfordshire

Since early Spring of 1917, the British Army was preparing its campaign in Palestine. On 1 October, General Allenby launched the British offensive by capturing Beersheva. On 9, December, General Allenby captured Jerusalem. The news was flashed around the world by wireless. Lloyd George sent a cable to Allenby: "War Cabinet wishes to congratulate you on the capture of Jerusalem, which is an event of historic and worldwide significance".

A few days later, in a letter to Herbert Samuel, Weizmann repudiated "...a rumour that a meeting took place between the Zionists and a representative of H.M. Government, at which it was decided that the Zionists relinquish every claim on Jerusalem".

Recruitment of Jewish volunteers for the Jewish Brigade was stepped up, with Major James de Rothschild in charge of enlistment in Palestine and Egypt. Three battalions joined Allenby on the Palestine Front. A British official reported that "practically the whole available Jewish youth in Palestine, whatever their national status, has enlisted". They were to be commended for their bravery by Gen. Clayton, Commander of Allenby's forces on the Eastern Front: "By forcing the Jordan fords, you helped in no small measure to win the great victory gained at Damascus" (October, 1918).

General Allenby entering Jerusalem

James de Rothschild
with Jewish recruits in Palestine

"Follow Him"

A State occasion

The British Government, ready to implement the principle of the Balfour Declaration, asked Weizmann to lead a Zionist Commission. On 8 March, 1918, on the eve of his departure for Palestine, Weizmann was presented to H.M. King George V at Buckingham Palace.

"I bought and put on my first and last top-hat," Weizmann recalled, and summing up that interview, Weizmann wrote: "He showed a great interest in our plans for Palestine". The boy from Motol had been vindicated. The English King had shown mercy! (see page 15).

The Jewish community in liberated Palestine greeted the arrival of the Zionist Commission with joy and emotion.

"We were received with fervent enthusiasm," Weizmann wrote to Vera, "and the trip, both to Jerusalem and around the colonies was a huge national holiday... It is sad, very sad in Jerusalem! The minarets and the bells and the domes rising to the sky, crying out that Jerusalem is not a Jewish city! There are few young Jews there, and the old ones are a dreadful sight. They are all broken off splinters, dusty, feeble, soft, covered with age-old mould... There's an enormous difference between what one sees in the colonies now and what there was to be seen eleven years ago when I was first here. In those days, they were sleepy villages, quite nice and neat, and now these settlements are so full of the

Arrival of the Zionist Commission at Lydda

65

joy of life that I've never seen such Jews before. And the children!... These children are absolutely blooming! The children are beautiful, natural, cheerful, they love the land..."

And about Tel Aviv, where he had stayed in a house owned by the Palestinian banker, Zalman David Levontin, in Yehuda Halevy Street, Weizmann wrote: "Tel Aviv is a little seaside town, consisting of perhaps a hundred houses and a few hundred inhabitants... quiet, almost desolate in its sand-dunes, cut off from the rest of the world for nearly four years."

In a letter to Mr. Justice Brandeis, Weizmann wrote: "Mr. Balfour's pronouncement came as a bombshell to the people both in Egypt and in Palestine... the sight of a colony with its strong and healthy young generation of fresh and beautiful children, singing and playing in Hebrew, was indeed inspiring... it is something quite new, Mr. Brandeis, and still the dignity of ancient history floats over the modest, but clean villages set up by our people. The Talmudic peasant is not a legend, but a living reality."

Weizmann stayed in Palestine for five months. One of the highlights of his tour of the country was a meeting with Emir Feisal, at Amman in the desert, at the suggestion of General Allenby.

Weizmann, his sister Gita, and Israel Sieff in Palestine

Weizmann, Allenby and the two Chief Rabbis in Jerusalem

Reception for the Zionist Commission in Rishon-Le-Zion

On the way to laying the foundation stones of the Hebrew University on Mt. Scopus

Welcoming the Zionist Commission in one of the plantation colonies

Weizmann addressing farmers

From Jerusalem, Weizmann travelled "by rail to Suez, then by boat to Akaba, circumventing the Sinai Peninsula, and from Akaba northward to Ma'an by such means of locomotion as might offer themselves. Thus the journey which today can be made in about half a day by car from Jerusalem took upward of ten days, and in the heat of June it was no pleasure jaunt", Weizmann was to recall, some twenty years later.

In a letter to Balfour after the meeting with Feisal, Weizmann wrote: "I foresee — and Feisal and his counsellors fully agree on this point — a possibility for sincere cooperation between the two nations... we shall come to his help, not as exploiters or concessionaries, but with a sincere desire to cooperate with a race which is destined to hold an important position in the Middle East".

Another highlight was the laying of twelve corner stones, representing the twelve tribes of Israel, for the erection of the Hebrew University on Mount Scopus. It took place in the presence of Allenby.

Weizmann's own description of the ceremony is romantic: "The declining sun flooded the hills of Judea and Moab with golden light, and it seemed to me, too, that the transfigured heights were watching, wandering, dimly aware that this was the beginning of the return of their own people after many days...".

The thousands of Jews who met him at Victoria Station, London, on his return from Palestine, in October, 1918 represented millions of Jews around the world, who were hailing Weizmann as the spokesman for the reborn nation in the councils of the nations. He led the Zionist delegations to the Peace Conferences — to the Peace Conferences at Versailles in 1919 and at San Remo in 1920.

Weizmann conducted himself as a statesman, in public appearances, in private meetings and in correspondence, even

if, as he said, "I have no army and no navy to back me up."
He was not even titular leader of the Zionist movement, his
election as President of the World Zionist Organisation being
confirmed only in 1921, at the first post-war Zionist Congress.

By 1919, Weizmann was expressing his prophetic inter-
pretation of contemporary Jewish history. In a letter to
General Money, Chief Administrator of the Occupied Enemy
Territory Administration (the British regime in Palestine) he
wrote: "The lesson which Jewry has learnt in the last few
terrible years has forced them to a conclusion that unless they
secure a place which they may call their home in a real
sense of the word, they will be faced by a terrible catastrophe.
Moreover, such a catastrophe would shatter not only the
whole fabric of Jewish existence but would endanger the
peace of society as a whole. This is, I am afraid, an incon-
trovertible fact whose tragic significance is not quite clear
to everybody. It was not quite evident even to myself,
because I also had the good fortune to live and work in
England. It is only recently, since the evil of war has been
slightly lifted, that the whole tragedy of my people has
become more apparent to me and it is their cry for help, their
just claim to exist, their wish, dictated by a relentless logic
of cruel facts, that I have tried to embody in this document.
God knows that this has not been done in any spirit of
arrogance or lust for power, not in a desire to do injustice to
other people!"

*The "Big Four" at the Peace
Conference — Lloyd George,
Clemenceau, Orlando and Wilson*

Meeting Emir Feisal in Ma'an near 'Aqaba

Observations he made when in Palestine in 1918, led Weizmann to warn the Zionists: "We ourselves are a national movement, and if there is a national movement among the Arabs, we must regard it earnestly".

On 3 January 1919, Weizmann and Emir Feisal signed an agreement, in Paris, drawn up by Col. T.E. Lawrence ('Lawrence of Arabia'), that spoke of "the closest possible collaboration in the development of the Arab State and Palestine", and of measures "to encourage and facilitate the immigration of Jews into Palestine on a large scale."

In spite of the subsequent repudiation of that agreement, Weizmann maintained, towards the end of his life that "the meeting in the desert laid the foundations of a lifelong friendship". Feisal, in March, 1919, wrote to the American Zionist leader, Felix Frankfurter: "With the chiefs of your movement, especially with Dr. Weizmann, we have had, and continue to have the closest relations".

Weizmann returned to Palestine in the autumn of 1919, this time accompanied by his wife and found "the first chalutzim arriving from the broken Jewish communities of Poland and other countries of Central and Eastern Europe. Some of them came with a rudimentary training in agriculture; others brought nothing but their devotion and their bare hands".

"In Palestine," Weizmann recorded, "I found myself obsessed by the discrepancy between the desirable and the possible. Occasionally, the difficulties — political and economic

Bringing the grapes to Rishon

alike — seemed so formidable that I felt a prey to dejection. Then I would go away alone into the hills or down to the seashore near Tel Aviv, to talk with some of the older settlers — men like Abraham Shapiro of Petach Tikvah, or Joshua Chankin" *(Yehoshua Hankin)* who acquired tracts in the Jezreel Valley for the Jewish National Fund in 1909, "or others of their generation. They would tell me of their own early difficulties when they had first come to the desert... they showed me the places that were already cultivated, covered with Jewish orange groves and vineyards... Rehovoth, Rishon-le-Zion — Petach Tikvah, so much had been done with limited means, limited experience, limited manpower, in this country."

After another hectic round of consultations and negotiations in London and Paris, Weizmann returned once more to Palestine, in March, 1920. This time, he took with him his 12 year-old son, Benjie, to visit Weizmann's mother, living in Haifa since her flight from Russia.

Weizmann and his son did not get up to Haifa for the Passover holiday. The atmosphere in Jerusalem, where they were staying, was ominous. Weizmann wrote to his Zionist colleagues in London: "I hasten to warn you of the very serious position which I have found on arrival here. Things have gone from bad to worse. Feisal is in the long run a broken reed. I can see other forces coming up which will break all he is connected with, break the European influence..."

In April, Arabs rioted in Jerusalem. Weizmann cabled to the British Prime Minister, Lloyd George: "Jerusalem where anti-Jewish excesses did not happen since the Crusades has been for three days the scene of wild pogroms, massacres, looting and violating of Jewish women".

The tension had been building up for some months. In Weizmann's words: "Lawless bands prowled and raided on our northern hills, and as is usual in such cases, banditry took on an aspect of patriotism. A month before, Joseph Trumpeldor, one of the earliest and greatest of the *chalutz* leaders, had gone up with some companions to the defence of Tel Hai, an infant colony near the Syrian border, and there he and five companions, two of them women, were killed by marauders."

Leaving from Plymouth for America, 1921

Weizmann described the attack on the Jews of Jerusalem "which seemed to have caught them completely unawares, and practically no resistance was offered. When one small group of young men, under Captain (Vladimir) Jabotinsky, had come out to defend their quarter, they had been promptly arrested... in the trials which followed before a military court, Jabotinsky received the savage sentence of fifteen years hard labour. He was later amnestied... but rejected the amnesty with scorn, because it included the main instigator of the pogrom, Amin el Husseini, the notorious Grand Mufti of later years, and one or two others of the same type. He insisted on making his appeal, and the sentence was in due course quashed."

The British Military Occupation ended within a few months of the riots of that Spring of 1920. Herbert Samuel, appointed first High Commissioner, took office on 1 July.

"Samuel will encounter not only difficulties with the Arabs, and not only have to struggle with the legacy which the old Administration will have left him, but he will meet with the bad spirit among our own people..." Weizmann predicted, in a letter to Dr. Eder in Jerusalem, then Acting Chairman of the Zionist Commission, in Palestine.

Returning to London, Weizmann had an internal Zionist political fight on his hands — the struggle for control of the World Zionist Organisation between the 'Americans', led by

The Mufti surrounded by his followers in Jerusalem

*The arrival of
the first High Commissioner,
Jaffa, 1920*

The landing of
Sir H. Samuel
at Jaffa
30-6-20

Congress Hall, Carlsbad, 1921

Mr. Justice Brandeis and the 'Europeans' led by Dr. Chaim Weizmann. The popular slogan was "Washington versus Pinsk". Victory went to the 'Europeans', but it was not until 1921, at the XIIth. Zionist Congress in Carlsbad, that Weizmann's personal victory was acknowledged, with his formal election as President of the World Zionist Organisation.

"From time to time there is a gleam of light. There is hope that... something will begin to move and will come to life in Palestine", he said at the time, and he had faith in the vision of two dynamic colleagues, Arthur Ruppin, an economist, who had been living for many years in the *Yishuv* and directed his efforts at viable colonisation of the country, and Pinkas Ruttenberg, who had escaped from Russia after the fall of Kerensky in 1917, and had conceived the hydro-electric project to harness the waters of the Jordan and Yarmuk. Weizmann was instrumental in obtaining the permission of the British Government for Ruttenberg to proceed with the imaginative scheme of the Palestine Electric Corporation.

"It is difficult to describe my impressions now," Weizmann wrote to Vera Weizmann, when he returned to Jerusalem in January, 1921. The newest thing, of course, are the immigrants working on the roads and organised in camps... they are obviously very good material, ready for many sacrifices. These people will be ready to break stones if they only know that one day they will be able to stand on the soil of Palestine and work it with their own plough". Two years later, when he had read Knut Hamsun's "The Growth of The Soil", which told the story of a Norwegian peasant who had broken stones to work on his land with his plough,

A festive gathering in Tel Aviv

Building the land — clearing stones

"Chalutzim" — Pioneers

77

Chaim Weizmann 1921

Vera Weizmann 1921

Weizmann wrote to Vera: "That magnificent man Izak (hero of Hamsun's novel) — when will we produce men like that?"

Winston Churchill, appointed British Colonial Secretary in 1921, immediately undertook a tour of the Middle East, which was to have fateful consequences for the region.

Weizmann, preparing for his first visit to the United States, was confident that Churchill would not be misled by Arab propaganda. On 10, March, he wrote to Herbert Samuel: "Hostile critics persistently accuse the immigrants of Bolshevik tendencies. Any prejudice that these charges may have created in Mr. Churchill's mind will be effectively dissipated by actual contacts with *chalutzim*".

Churchill planting a tree on Mt. Scopus, 1921, with Herbert Samuel

Three months later, Churchill stated in the House of Commons: "I defy anybody, after seeing work of this kind (the vineyards and the orange groves of the *Yishuv*) achieved by so much labour, effort and skill to say that the British Government, having taken up the position it has, could cast it all aside and leave it to be brutally overturned by the incursion of a fanatical attack by the Arab population from outside".

Reception held by Sir Herbert and Lady Samuel (left) at Government House for Colonial Secretary Winston Churchill and wife (right), also attended by Emir Abdullah of Transjordan

Churchill speaks in Jerusalem

Troubled Palestine

The fanatical attack, thus condemned by Churchill, had occurred in May, 1921 when a Labour Day demonstration in Jaffa was turned by Arab rioters into a bloodbath, in which forty-seven Jews lost their lives. The principal Arab provocateur was Amin el Husseini, who, having been amnestied by Herbert Samuel, was nominated by the High Commissioner as Mufti of Jerusalem. His appointment perturbed Jews and moderates among the Arab population in Palestine, and was to cast a baleful influence on Arab-Jewish relations for many decades, even after he had been exiled (in 1937) from Palestine.

The Jaffa riots coincided with Weizmann's first visit to the United States. Louis Lipsky, whom Weizmann in a later assessment described as "The pillar of American Zionism", had invited him "to see for myself what could and what could not be done in America".

Weizmann went with two main objectives — "to found the American *Keren Hayesod* (Palestine Foundation Fund)... and to awaken American interest in the Hebrew University".

Prof. Albert Einstein was already an international figure and Weizmann asked a mutual friend, Kurt Blumenfeld to persuade Einstein to join the group.

"Weizmann represents Zionism," Blumenfeld recalled telling Einstein, "He alone can make decisions. He is the President of our Organisation, and if you take your conversion to Zionism seriously, then I have the right to ask you, in Dr. Weizmann's name, to go with him to the United States and to do what he at the moment thinks is necessary".

Einstein responded positively. He told a mass rally of over 5000 enthusiastic Jews in New York, on 12 April 1921:

The Zionist Conference in London
which established the Keren Hayesod

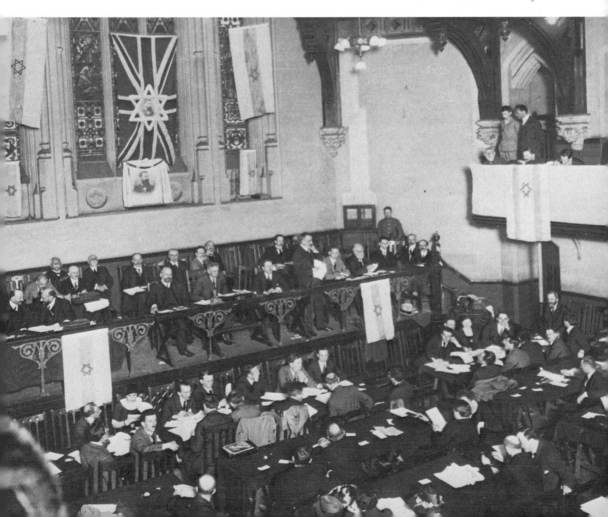

*Dr. and Mrs. Weizmann with Prof. and Mrs.
Albert Einstein, Menahem Ussishkin (left)
and Dr. Benzion Mossinson (right),
in the United States, April, 1921*

"Our leader and your leader, Dr. Weizmann has spoken, and spoken very well, for us all. He has rendered great service to the Jewish people. Follow him and you will do well. That is all I have to say".

Later that year, Einstein was awarded the Nobel Prize. On arrival in the U.S. with Weizmann, he was asked to explain his Theory of Relativity. "If you will not take the answer too seriously, and consider it only as a kind of joke, then I can explain it as follows," he replied, "It was formerly believed that if all material things disappeared out of the universe, time and space would be left. According to the Relativity Theory, time and space disappear together with the things".

Leaving an official reception
at New York City Hall, 1921

Weizmann and Einstein were guests of President Harding in Washington and were feted wherever they spoke.

"I have just got a new theory of eternity", Einstein quipped after a series of formal welcome addresses. "During our voyage," Weizmann told reporters in New York, "Einstein explained his theory to me every day and on my arrival I am fully convinced that he understands it!"

Their triumphant tour was marred by the news of the May Day massacre in Jaffa. From Toronto, Weizmann sent this message to a mass meeting of protest by Chicago Jewry:

"Jews have once more fallen victims to unprovoked assaults of Arab fanaticism. The events that have occurred in Jaffa represent a renewed attempt at intimidation... If Jewish blood has been shed, it is for the Jewish people to see that it shall not be shed in vain. For every Jew who has fallen, a thousand newcomers must be brought in".

The High Commissioner greets the Mufti at Government House, Jerusalem

Weizmann and Sir Alfred Mond visiting Bezalel School of Art

Reception for Weizmann
in Washington, D.C.

"The Brandeis group is frightened of international Zionism because it is linked up with England. As long as the Wilson regime lasted they were protected. Under the present regime, which is not altogether favourable to England, they would like to impart to Zionism *an American stamp*... the Jewish masses who are nationalist Jews worry little about such things. They are primarily interested in Palestine... in their arguments against the *Keren Hayesod* the Brandeis Group stated that American money must not go out into a country under a British mandate. The American Zionist leaders are also frightened of Henry Ford and his propaganda and would therefore like to hide their Jewish lights under a bushel..." Weizmann, in a letter to Sir Alfred Mond, in May 1921. At the American Zionist Convention, in Cleveland, a new pro-Weizmann leadership was elected.

In a letter to Sir Herbert Samuel in Palestine, Weizmann wrote:

"It was a bitter struggle but it is over now... we have now got to make up for it all and God willing and with your support we shall do it".

Tel Aviv, early '20's

תל-אביב—שכונת רוזנפלד
Tel-Aviv — Rosenfeld's Quarter

תל-אביב—שכונת צילנוב
Tel-Aviv — Tchlenov Quarter

Nahalal

"I have tried to pull up the political position and had heart to heart talks with Lloyd George, Balfour, Churchill, prolonged conferences with Smuts, with the Colonial Office people. When I look back on this terrible year and review what has happened in Palestine; we have got in 1000 immigrants, we have bought 100,000 dunam land, we are building about two hundred houses, about six factories are going up — all that in this most miserable of years with a pogrom, with a financial crisis, with America what it was—I take courage. If we only get a dog's chance, we shall do it alright" (from a letter by Weizmann to Abe Tulin, a friend and fellow Zionist in New York, in May 1921).

"You cannot build up Nahalal without National Funds," Weizmann told Jewish businessmen, when campaigning in America. "The *Chalutzim* are willing to miss meals twice a week. But cows must be fed, and you cannot feed a cow with speeches".

Throughout the Twenties, Weizmann's labours took him from London to Europe, the United States of America, and to Palestine. On one such voyage to the U.S., he travelled on the luxury French Liner s.s. "Paris", and his descriptions of the voyage, in letters to his wife, make amusing reading:

"The French crew of the "Paris" gave our launch some senseless orders. At long last, the English Captain of our launch lost patience and demanded that the Captain of the "Paris" should come and see for himself... after a lengthy exchange of insults, very typical of the *Entente Cordiale,* the Captain of the "Paris" put in an appearance and declared that it was very easy to fix a ladder and that should the English refuse to do this, he would leave the passengers to their fate and sail off. The poor passengers were by then so exhausted and frozen, so sick, that they would gladly have returned to Plymouth — I among them. At that moment, our small craft struck the "Paris" with such violence that even the Frenchman saw reason and decided to take his large ship into port..."

Salon of the s.s. Paris

The s.s. Paris

British public opinion was divided over the ratification of the Mandate and British obligations to the Jewish people. "Zionism at the present juncture is being persistently assailed from a variety of quarters", Weizmann wrote to Balfour in 1922, appealing to the British statesman for advice.

Weizmann himself became the butt of ridicule in some sections of the British Press, and was even the subject of a vicious smear campaign.

Arab propaganda, coupled with hostile articles in Anglican and Catholic journals, alerted Weizmann to new dangers.

In a letter to David Eder, at that time the senior Zionist representative in Palestine, Weizmann wrote:

"Our enemies in Palestine are not stopping at anything in order to destroy our position. They have already started the circulation of postcards with the Jewish flag on Mohammedan Holy Places... after the Mandate has been ratified, the Arabs may attempt a general rising in Palestine... they may try and tamper with the Holy Places and lay this at the door of the Jews".

Daily Express

,03J. LONDON, SATURDAY, OCTOBER 28. 1922.

Why We are Still in Palest.

MYSTERY OF THE GREAT CHAIM.

LAST OF THE FOREIGNERS WHO MEDDLE WITH BRITISH AFFAIRS.

PALESTINE MORASS.

GENIUS THAT LURED AND KEEPS US THERE.

Since the armistice our commitments in the Middle East have cost the British taxpayer £225,000,000 —nearly as much as the Boer war. That is the price paid by the British taxpayer for our adventures in Constantinople, Mesopotamia, and Palestine.

It is the genius of Dr. Chaim Weizmann, the Last of the Foreigners and most powerful of the Mystery Men that keeps us in Palestine.

NOVEMBER 3, 1922.

YOUR SAVINGS FOR A JEWISH STATE?

WHAT THE LABOUR PARTY WOULD DO WITH THEM.

SAFETY FIRST.

CLEAR OUT BAG AND BAGGAGE!

The Labour Party demand a capital levy on all savings over £5,000.

What do they propose to do with your savings?

Among other things they propose to pour them into the Palestine wastes.

The Right Hon. Arthur Henderson has declared that "the British

---

OCTOBER 30.

THE C AGAIN LLOYD GE

REASONS WHY EXPELLED OFFIC

SILENT LE

FAILURE TO A FIGH

THE Conservative the campaign a of the general elec servatives think th their place in front paign develops?

We believe that

Lawrence of Arabia

Support for Weizmann and the Zionists came from unexpected quarters. For instance Col. T.E. Lawrence reprimanded an Anglican Bishop in a letter to the London *'Times'*:

"Dr. Weizmann is a great man whose boots neither you, nor I, my dear Bishop, are fit to black".

The summer of 1922 brought mixed blessings to the Zionists. While the ratification of the Palestine Mandate by the Council of the League of Nations, in London, late in July — "up to the last day we were uncertain of what would happen", according to Weizmann — gave Weizmann cause for satisfaction — "with the unanimous vote for ratification there ended the first chapter of our long political struggle"— the publication of the Churchill White Paper on Palestine a month earlier gave Weizmann his first serious test of statesmanship as President of the World Zionist Organisation.

The White Paper of 1922 indicated to the Jews and the Arabs that the "Pax Britannica" would divide and rule them. It legalised the status of the land east of the Jordan — two-thirds of the country which at the time of the ratification of the Balfour Declaration at San Remo in 1920 was defined as 'Palestine' — as the Hashemite Kingdom of Transjordan. It confirmed that "the Jewish community was in Palestine as of right and not on sufferance".

Throughout the Jewish world, the White Paper was

assailed as a whittling down of the promise of the Balfour Declaration. Conscious that the Mandate itself was not a foregone conclusion, and that the Council of the League of Nations was due to vote on it within weeks, Weizmann reluctantly persuaded the Zionist Executive to give the British Colonial Office its assurance that "it was prepared to conduct its activities in conformity with the terms of the White Paper".

Frederick Kisch

Col. Kisch in Jerusalem

"There is another question bound up with the passing of the Mandate. After the ratification of the Mandate, the Zionist Organisation will be in a position to extend an invitation to men like Marshall, James de Rothschild and others to come into the Agency, and if we have a plan, that too would help bring this new blood into the orbit of real Palestine work, instead of applying itself only to the sporadic creation of companies," Weizmann wrote in a letter to a Zionist colleague, Emanuel Neumann of New York, in 1922.

Weizmann worked on that plan for seven years. Finally, the enlarged Jewish Agency was convened in Zurich, in 1929.

British troops in Palestine

Weizmann's home and the headquarters of the World Zionist Movement were now in London. He designated Col. Fred Kisch, appointed Political Adviser to the Zionist Executive in Palestine in 1923, to represent the Zionist Movement among the British, Arab and Foreign Officials in Palestine. "Kisch's arrival in Palestine meant much to me personally. For the first time there was somebody with whom to share the work... someone who could also go to America and talk to the assimilated Jews there as man to man... indeed he was better able to talk to them than I was..." Weizmann wrote.

At the XIIIth. Zionist Congress, in Carlsbad, in 1923, Weizmann was authorised to go ahead with his programme to bring in to the Jewish Agency non-Zionists on a partnership basis. His message was: "We have built and the world has destroyed. We have built again and the world has destroyed again... We had built in Babylon — it was destroyed; we had built in Spain — it was destroyed; we built in Eastern and Central Europe — and what is left today? Ruins, spiritual and physical. Our communities are shattered, the labour of generations has gone for nought. Again we must build, again we must return to beginnings. Zionism is our last desperate effort to ensure our sense of continuity".

Weizmann in Boston 1923

96

"It has fallen to my lot to adapt the Zionist Organisation to modern requirements, and if this process of adaptation is difficult, nobody suffers from it more than I do myself. It must not be forgotten that non-Zionist Jews form an integral part of the Jewish community, and it is our duty to carry them along with us, even if we can only take them part of the way". This letter to the Zionist Executive in London, written by Weizmann from New York, early in 1924, on the eve of the first conference of American Non-Zionist Jews, echoed a favourite theme.

"My life consists of short intervals between long trips..." Weizmann confided to Eric Mendelsohn, member of the *Bauhaus Group* of architects in Berlin, in a letter written early in 1925. Weizmann promised Mendelsohn he would send him "a sketch of our house to be built in Jerusalem". Mendelsohn would eventually build a house for the Weizmanns in Palestine, but on a hill in Rehovot. It was completed twelve years later.

Touring Palestine 1923

*A Labour conference in Tel Aviv, 1923; the ushers included
Yitzhak Ben-Zvi, David Ben-Gurion and Joseph Sprinzak*

*A personal memento given to
Weizmann, Allenby, Balfour and
Samuel, photographed together in
Jerusalem*

*Col. F.H. Kisch and members of the Zionist Executive
meet with Arab sheikhs (1925)*

Belfour

Herbert Samuel

Jerusalem
April 1925

"One of the most important events marking our progress since the Balfour Declaration is about to take place", Weizmann wrote in a letter to Lord Walter Rothschild, ... "Lord Balfour has consented to go out to Palestine to open the Hebrew University on 1 April (1925)... the ceremony will be incomplete without your presence, you to whom the Balfour Declaration was addressed". The oldest of the Rothschild's — then eighty — Baron Edmond de Rothschild, accepted Weizmann's invitation to "... participate in this unique event in Jewish history, an event for which you are so largely responsible".

Weizmann later recalled: "One event stands out in the decade of the 'twenties on which I linger with pleasure, both because of its practical and its symbolic significance... the opening of the Hebrew University".

Welcoming Lord Balfour, April 1925

A formal portrait of the Weizmanns, Balfour and Nahum Sokolow

At the opening of the Hebrew University on Mt. Scopus

Balfour visiting Tel Aviv and escorted by Sokolow, Dizengoff, Warburg, Weizmann and others

תל-אביב—שכונת הפקידים
Tel-Aviv—The Clerks' Quarter

Early postcard views of Tel Aviv

תל-אביב—לב תל-אביב
Tel-Aviv — Lev-Tel-Aviv

תל-אביב—רחוב השחר
Tel-Aviv — Hashahar Str.

Relaxing in Wiesbaden with Mrs Landsberg,
her children and Leonard Stein

It was a decisive decade for Weizmann, for Zionism and for Palestine, a decade of set-backs and achievements.

"There is a great moral strength in our people; this strength is covered by layers of slag and can only be revealed through a process of intense purification. It is a long and painful path and only the few have taken it, but those few will eventually achieve it and will raise the others up again", Weizmann wrote to Leonie Landsberg, wife of Dr. Arthur Landsberg, prominent German Jewish leader and Zionist, in January, 1925.

"Last night I was at the Einsteins. He is just as wonderful as ever. All the intelligentsia of Berlin was there. The general mood here is quite good. People work very hard and will achieve something. Germany will become a powerful factor again. Jews have a hard time here and this is apparent in everything. They are rather subdued", from a letter to Vera Weizmann from Berlin, written in January, 1925.

Weizmann derived inspiration for his indefatigable speech-making in the United States and Europe, from the immigrants who began in the early twenties to come from the small towns of Eastern Europe to farm in Palestine. He was disturbed by the trend of the middle class *Aliyah* (immigration) in the period from 1924 to 1926, known as the "Grabski Aliyah", after the Polish Government whose anti-Jewish legislation had motivated it.

Overleaf – Balfour addressing the
assembly at the official opening
of the Hebrew University on Mt.
Scopus in April, 1925

Informal discussions between Sir Herbert Samuel and Officers in Palestine

*The second High Commissioner to Palestine, Field-Marshal
Lord Plumer and wife at the opening of the Agricultural
Exhibition in Haifa, 1927*

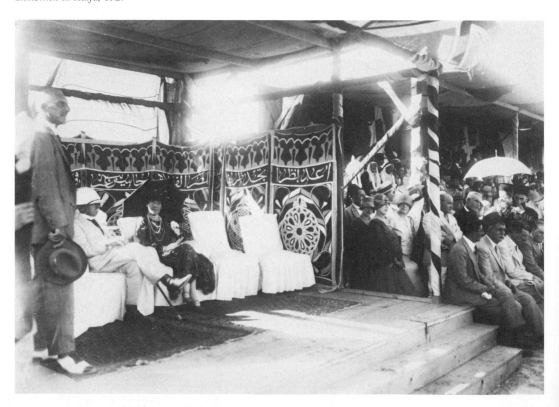

Samuel's impending departure viewed in a Purim satirical
publication, HaDorban (The Spur), Jerusalem, titled "Five
Years Later..." — Rabbi Israel — "with you, it was bad,
without you, it will be worse": Uncle Ishmael — "thanks to
you, we can hold our heads high"

"...If we in Palestine will build up towns, and the land and the hinterland of these towns will not be Jewish in the sense that it will be worked and tilled and laboured by Jewish effort, we may repeat the fatal experiment (of the Jews of Warsaw) and the same fatal results which have happened in Poland will be repeated in Tel Aviv... if we shall not establish a balance between the growth of the town and the growth of the Jewish village, we shall repeat the same fatal mistakes we have made all over the world... there is no room in Palestine for a skyscraper. It will make Palestine top-heavy and the structure will topple over and crush us all." Weizmann told a mass rally in Carnegie Hall, New York on 16 February, 1925.

The building boom in Palestine came to an end in the spring of 1926. A recession which was to blight the land until 1929 set in, resulting in unemployment, hunger and eventually, Jewish emigration. The Zionist leadership was bitter about lost opportunities and frustrated aspirations for the fledgeling homeland.

"When Nehemia was building up Palestine, he was besieged on all sides — Tobias wanted to destroy the Declaration of King Cyrus. Palestine was poor, ruined. The rich men remained in Babylon, gave a little money and sent only the poor people. *They* were building with their blood, dying of starvation, but nevertheless built up, created a language, purified the people from idolatry, saved the Torah and kept it for us. *Plus ça change, c'est la même chose"*, Weizmann wrote to Hannah Rovina, in New York, in 1927.

A visit to Palestine in 1928, by the Habimah Hebrew Theatre Group which had left Moscow for Europe and the United States two years earlier, lit up the general gloom of the *Yishuv* at that time.

"I am certain that the decision of Habimah to remain in America is senseless and will lead to a complete failure. If one is to die,... then at least with honour and dignity in Palestine. And I am sure that there is a future there. The crisis is not going to last forever, and we shall see better days," Weizmann wrote to Hannah Rovina, a leading actress of the Habimah Group, in June 1927. "I can recommend only one thing, to leave America and go to Palestine... it is true that it is difficult in Palestine at present, but the difficulties there are better than the American 'easiness'..."

"The unemployment is a disease very difficult to cure and can hardly be dealt with, without a substantial loan. I saw

Hannah Rovina's affectionate tribute to Weizmann on the day she describes as "Jewish Agency Day"

Poincare. He definitely promised me that France would participate in a loan. Of course England must take the initiative. I saw Balfour before I left and he declared that after Amery's return, he was prepared to call a conference (Amery, Churchill, Balfour and our representatives) to discuss the situation in Palestine", Weizmann — in a letter to Arthur and Leonie Landsberg, in Berlin, at the beginning of January, 1928.

"We have reduced the dole now in Tel Aviv to two thousand from three thousand six hundred. This is not merely seasonal, but there is a real improvement in the situation", Weizmann reported in a letter to Oskar Wasserman, in Berlin, in February, 1928.

Ruppin and Weizmann at the XVIth Zionist Congress, Zurich, 1929

Sir John Chancellor, the third High Commissioner to Palestine, awarding Honours on the King's Birthday

Dissident voices were increasingly raised against Weizmann's authority to speak on behalf of the Zionist leadership in Palestine. The economic strain, the Arab threats, the vacillations of an unsympathetic High Commissioner, Sir John Chancellor, who had succeeded Sir Herbert Samuel and Field-Marshal Lord Plumer, dismayed and confused Zionist spokesmen.

"It must be left entirely to me to judge whether I have given false hopes to *chalutzim* or not... I was besieged by hundreds of young men (in Rumania) and I told them for the present there is not emigration into, but rather an immigration out of Palestine", Weizmann wrote in sharp protest against doubts expressed by his Zionist colleague, Harry Sacher, in Jerusalem, about the wisdom of speeches Weizmann was making in Europe at that time.

"The speech in Czernowitz was actually not a speech but an attempt to reveal the inner motives that activate one... sometimes I feel as if everything is easy and it needs only goodwill to progress — then I sprout wings. Sometimes (and that is very often), I plunge into despair..." from a letter to M. Spiegel, a colleague in Berlin, 24 April, 1928, and "I am convinced that America is moving further and away from European civilisation... a robot race of modern Redskins is

111

"Black Friday," Wall Street, 1929

emerging, armed with tremendous power. Poor Western Europe is exposed to pressure of two currents; Russia with too much heart and nerves, America without heart and nerves", he wrote in the same letter.

"....My plans are not yet absolutely clear, but I am probably going to America in October for a month; in the winter, I hope to stay either at home or in Zurich, where I want to start some chemical work. This last year has been very difficult; the troubles in Palestine drove me all over the world and didn't leave me in peace anywhere,... I shall serve the Movement this year, and I already want to start gradually going back to my chemical activities..." from a letter Weizmann wrote on 29, August, 1928 to his mother, sister and brothers in Palestine.

By the summer of 1928, it was evident that the Jewish National Home had survived the economic crisis. The "Great Depression", ushered in by the Wall Street stock market crash on 'Black Friday,' October 29, 1929, was to blight the prospects for a big upsurge in the *Yishuv's* economic development, envisaged by Weizmann's "extended Jewish Agency" plan, brought to successful finality in August, 1929.

Weizmann had worked patiently to implement the programme he had presented to the Zionist Congress in 1922. A dedicated and able Zionist leadership in America, headed by Louis Lipsky had given him loyal support, and the two pivotal American Jews from the ranks of the non-Zionists in the drawn-out campaign to reach an agreement were Louis Marshall, influential and charismatic, and Felix Warburg, "public-spirited and the *grand seigneur*", as Weizmann described him.

They endorsed Weizmann's view, expressed in 1928, that "The Balfour Declaration was given not to the Zionists alone but to the Jewish people as a whole; and the entire people must accept it with clean hands and a pure heart".

The first meeting of the enlarged Jewish Agency, which took place in Zurich on 11 August, 1929, was festive, a demonstration of Jewish solidarity much more impressive than the First Zionist Congress, which Herzl had convened thirty-two years earlier.

Some members of the 1927–1929 Zionist Executive; seated, Henrietta Szold, Weizmann, David Eder; standing (l. to r.), Harry Sacher, Siegfried van Vriesland and F.H. Kisch

Ханнѣ Роввиной, моему дорогому другу
Великой артистки и великой выразительницы еврейского пафоса и еврейской
трагедіи с глубоким поэтическим преклонениемъ
и любовью отъ Хаимъ Вейцманнъ

New York, Пурим 1927 г.

Weizmann, New York, 1927

On the main table with Dr. Weizmann were his veteran colleagues, Sokolow and Ussishkin; Sir Herbert Samuel, first High Commissioner for Palestine, Prof. Albert Einstein, Nobel Prize laureate; Lord Melchett, the British industrialist who had cooperated with Weizmann on important Palestinian projects for several years; Leon Blum the French statesman; Louis Marshall; Sir Osmond d'Avigdor-Goldsmid, a prominent leader of Anglo-Jewry, Oscar Wasserman, a German Jewish financier; and Sholem Asch, the most famous Jewish writer of his time.

The buoyancy of the Jewish Assembly meeting gave way to what Weizmann described as "a series of dark events." Weizmann recalled the sequence of events thus: "A few days after the Constituent Assembly had dispersed amid mutual felicitations, and while Zionists and non-Zionists all over the world were congratulating themselves on the creation of this new and powerful instrument of Jewish action, the Palestine riots broke out on 23 August. On 11, September, Louis Marshall, the mainstay of the non-Zionist section of the Agency, died after an operation. And within a few weeks, there came the great economic crash of 1929, to be followed by the long depression — perhaps the severest in modern history — which struck hard at the sources of support which the Agency had planned to tap."

Louis Marshall

Samuel Untermeyer

Felix Warburg

Sir Alfred Mond (later Lord Melchett)

Dangerous Decade

"'The Under Secretary of State regrets to announce...' were the first words of the cable which brought me the news of the Palestine pogroms of 1929, in which nearly a hundred and fifty Jews were killed, hundreds more wounded, and great property damage done. I was struck as by a thunderbolt. This then was the answer of the Arab leadership... they had realised that our fortunes had taken an upward turn... the way to prevent that, they thought, — wrongly, as we all know now — was a blood-bath". Thus Weizmann recalled how in his short holiday in the Bernese Alps was interrupted by the news of the massacre in Hebron and the riots in Jerusalem, Jaffa, Safad and several rural settlements.

Weizmann reacted to these blows with courage: "The late events have proved that not a single Jew in Palestine has been shaken. The Jews in London and New York are more frightened than the Jews of Jerusalem... no amount of pogroms will frighten us... we are in Palestine and we shall stay", Weizmann told the Anglo-Palestine Club in London, in December, 1929, but privately he expressed his misgivings to Sir Herbert Samuel: "Difficulties take a long time to solve, the impossible always takes a little longer!"

Relations with the British Government were rapidly deteriorating, due in no small measure to the anti-Zionist views of the Colonial Secretary of the Labour Government, Lord Passfield, whose wife, formerly Beatrice Webb asked "Why do the Jews make such a fuss over a few dozen of their people killed in Palestine. As many are killed every

London, 1928. Preparing for the enlarged Jewish Agency

Destruction in Hulda in the wake of the Arab riots, 1929

The Great Synagogue in Hebron, desecrated in the riots of 1929

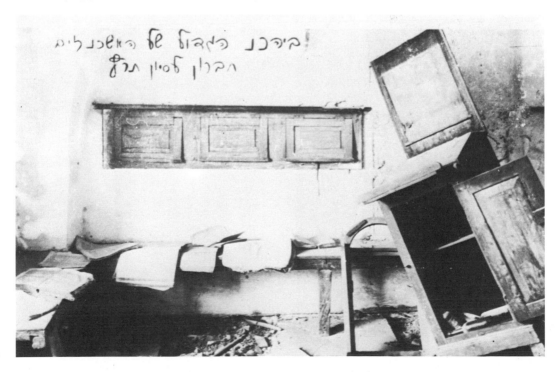

A troubled Prime Minister —
Ramsay MacDonald, 1931

Sidney Webb (Lord Passfield)

Beatrice Webb

week in London in traffic accidents, and no one pays any attention." Two unfavourable official British reports, that of the Shaw Commission on the causes of the 1929 Arab onslaughts and by Sir John Hope Simpson on the immigration policy for Palestine were not unexpected by Weizmann, but a breach of promise by Prime Minister Ramsay MacDonald, in connection with the Passfield White Paper of October, 1930, provoked Weizmann to declare "One thing the Jews will never forgive, and that is having been fooled!"

In his intense struggle with the Colonial Office, Weizmann rallied around him many prominent English personalities, one of whom, Mrs. Blanche 'Baffy' Dugdale was to serve for a decade as a member of Weizmann's political entourage at 77 Great Russell Street, London.

Powerful figures in British and Imperial politics joined in the Jewish protest against the Passfield White Paper, men of the calibre of Stanley Baldwin, General Smuts, Sir Austen Chamberlain, Leopold Amery, Sir John Simon, Lord Reading, Lord Melchett, and Lloyd George.

Blanche Dugdale ("Baffy")

As a gesture of personal protest, Weizmann resigned the Presidency of the Jewish Agency, in October 1930. The house of Commons debate on the "White Paper" indicated that British public opinion was not prepared to countenance a surrender of the British policy on a Jewish National Home to Arab violence and intransigence. On 13 February, 1931, Ramsay MacDonald sent Weizmann a letter which was conciliatory in tone but ambiguous in substance over the recommendations of the "White Paper". The Arabs angrily referred to MacDonald's letter as "The Black Letter" substituting for the "White Paper"!

Weizmann maintained that "irrespective of its form as a document, the Letter rectified the situation". This letter — and Weizmann's assessment of it, which he made public — was to play an important role in the first major setback Weizmann was to suffer at the hands of his Zionist colleagues, later that year.

"I don't like to hide it from you, but it did me a world of good to hear from you that some of the younger generation feel a certain attachment to me. It was doubly welcome as I mean to go out very soon. This is naturally a wrench for me. It sometimes aches and your words were and are a comfort — perhaps the younger people will begin to assert themselves sooner than I thought... The negotiations with H.M. Government will probably be completed in another fortnight. I shall consider myself a free man then, and shall begin to think of

The Weizmanns with Chaim Arlosoroff, Political Secretary of the Jewish Agency and Dr Itzhak Wilkansky (Elazari-Volcani) in Rehovot

Lloyd George replying to toast in his honour on the occasion of his 70th. birthday at a Banquet, Savoy Hotel, London, 1933

Chemistry", Weizmann wrote on 26 April, 1931 to Herbert Samuel's son, Edwin at that time a civil servant in the British Colonial Office.

The Seventeenth Zionist Congress met in Basel in July 1931 in an implacable mood, determined that "if they cannot throw the British Government out, they will throw Chaim Weizmann out instead!". In his opening address, Weizmann had announced his intention to resign, but his political foes sought a vote of no confidence in his policy.

"We are creating Palestine, and not another hand has touched what we have done there. This is our title to nobility, and our title to a place in the world... the walls of Jericho fell at the blowing of trumpets, but I have never heard of walls having been erected by such means!" Weizmann told the turbulent Congress delegates. The crucial vote went against Weizmann. The closing session was convened with Weizmann no longer on the rostrum.

"Suddenly two ushers opened a side door and the figure of Weizmann, tall and stately, his expression grave, emerged... slowly and in measured steps, he walked at the head of the group of Labour Zionist delegates to the left wing of the hall...

the atmosphere became electric. An ovation began, spreading in waves from the galleries to the hall and thence to the platform. Soon the whole Congress was engulfed in it. Weizmann remained seated. The applause gathered volume and continued until he was compelled to rise from his seat. It was the signal for a renewed acclamation. Delegates wept and in effusive Continental fashion embraced and kissed each other. Weizmann was not elected President of the World Zionist Organisation at that Congress. In the moment of his defeat, he was anointed the leader of his people," Meyer Weisgal, then a newspaper correspondent, cabled to his journal in Toronto.

After the vote of no confidence, Jabotinsky, who had led the opposition to Weizmann before and during the congress, sent Vera Weizmann a note "I am proud of my friends", to which she replied "Thanks for condolences. We are not dead yet!"

Weizmann's concluding words to that Congress were:

"We Jews have always had to suffer from being misunderstood. Zionism and its realisation in Palestine is an attempt to remove this misunderstanding. It is perhaps one of the greatest of our difficulties, and it would be naive to believe that ten years of work suffice to overcome such obstacles. I do not believe that Palestine can be attained through a short cut. What I believe is that we shall attain our National Home through hard, tedious and deep suffering. We are all bound up together in strong faith in the Zionist idea and its realisation. But deep faith in a cause is not manifested through heroic phrases but through the patience with which daily difficulties are met. In this spirit we must continue on our way without hesitation..."

At last Weizmann felt free to accept a long-standing invitation to visit South Africa. In the course of a tour which took them across the length and the breadth of the country, the Weizmann's formed many lasting friendships. Dr. Weizmann, campaigning with Dr. Alexander Goldstein, raised some hundred thousand pounds sterling for the *Keren Hayesod*.

Met in New York by Judge Morris Rothenberg, Louis Lipsky and Meyer Weisgal

Visiting South Africa with Vera
and Dr Alexander Goldstein, 1932

"With all the difficulties in their way, the Jews have demonstrated that Palestine could be built up and that Jews could build it up. They conducted their work by the strength of a great ideal. This ideal moved the earth and a little of heaven. It produced a new breed of men as if by a miracle", Weizmann told an audience in Bloemfontein, South Africa.

"The South African Jews were kindly, hard-working, intelligent people, and what one may term organic Zionists. It was a pleasure to watch and hear those Jews" Weizmann recalled.

"On Safari"

Mayoral reception at Benoni in the Transvaal

The rise of the Nazi Reich came at a time when Weizmann was nominally out of office in the World Zionist Organisation. With anti-Semitism threatening to engulf European Jewry, and the Jewish National Home under physical attack in Palestine from the Arabs, and at a low political ebb in British Government circles, it was to Weizmann that the Zionist movement — and world Jewry — turned once more for effective leadership.

"I could not see my way for strong moral reasons to accept the Presidency (of the World Zionist Organisation), under the conditions that prevailed (at the XVIIIth. Zionist Congress in Prague in 1933), Weizmann wrote to Swiss scientist, Prof. Fritz Haber, later in that fateful year — "but I have gladly undertaken to do an important and difficult piece of work — perhaps the most important piece of work in the Movement today — and I do not want to be shackled by the day-to-day routine work of the Zionist Organisation or to be a butt for the critical attack of people who are blinded by party animosities... I hope to carry on with my work independently and unhampered."

Essentially his work was the rescue of German Jewry, and their settlement, as far as the restrictions of the Mandatory Power would allow, in Palestine. He negotiated with political leaders and public-spirited men of all nations, he maintained personal contacts with refugees and with Jews still in Germany, he improved relief, created work opportunities, especially for the academically-trained, inaugurated retraining and colonisation schemes. He addressed hundreds of meetings, wrote countless letters, travelled tirelessly to rally Jewish and general support for Hitler's victims.

Hitler — a German placard, 1933

Weizmann with Zionist youth in Czechoslovakia, 1933

Weizmann had intended to resume his work in chemistry. Approaching sixty, he found that it required "a psychological effort to revert to quiet laboratory work — I had not been in a laboratory, except on a chance visit, for about thirteen years after the stormy and adventurous life of the preceding years... I had lost contact with practical work... to restart this sort of professional occupation in one's mature years is painful and difficult... but quite suddenly, and unexpectedly, there came to my assistance, Professor Richard Willstatter, one of the greatest modern chemists, who had come to London (from Germany) to receive the Gold Medal of the Royal Society... he agreed that we should collaborate in a field which was very familiar to him... I took over only a small corner of this vast field, and was able to make something practical of it — a vegetable foodstuff... Willstatter was consistently helpful to me... I was urged on by two factors. First, my intrinsic relation to science which had been part of my life since my boyhood; second, my feeling that in one way or another it had something to do with the building of Palestine".

Nobel Prize winner, Prof. Richard Willstatter at the opening of the Daniel Sieff Institute, Rehovot, 1934

At a time when, in Willstatter's words: "The German nation gave free play to the rawest predatory and cruel anti-Semitism, whose pre-requisite was the consent and toleration of thousands who sought advantage and millions who were weak and cowardly, and the universities and learned societies were outstanding in their weakness from the very beginning...", Weizmann, as he confessed later, "found it impossible, in those years of crisis — as in fact I had found it impossible in an earlier crisis, that which followed the Kishinev and other pogroms thirty years before — to abstract myself even temporarily from Jewish life".

Responding to a call from Meyer Weisgal, who was producing "Romance Of A People" in Chicago, Weizmann made an 8000 miles journey for a single appearance which drew some 150,000 people, breaking all attendance records at the Chicago World's Fair. "I accepted Weisgal's offer for the sake of the Central Refugee Fund and out of regard for the man", Weizmann wrote. Weisgal summed up the triumphant Weizmann visit thus: "He was still out of office, but his name was still magic!"

This placard calling for a total boycott of Jewish enterprises posted on Jewish business premises on 1 April, 19 heralded the Nazi persecution of Jews

Zur Abwehr!

Am 30. Januar 1933 wurde **Adolf Hitler**, der Führer der deutschen Freiheitsbewegung, zum Kanzler des Deutschen Reiches ernannt. Am 5. März 1933 bekannte sich das deutsche Volk in einer wunderbaren Erhebung zu ihm und zu seinem Befreiungswerk. Die

nationale Revolution

schlug das alte System in Trümmer, der Marxismus liegt zerschmettert am Boden, Deutschland geht einem neuen Aufstieg entgegen.

Dieser grandiose deutsche Freiheitskampf erfüllt den

internationalen Weltjuden

mit Haß und Grimm. Er sieht, daß es mit seiner Macht in Deutschland zu Ende geht. Er sieht, aus **diesem** Deutschland kann er keine sowjetjüdische Verbrecherkolonie mehr machen. Jetzt handelt er nach dem Programm, das der jüdische Zionistenführer **Theodor Herzl** im Jahre 1897 in Basel bei einem großen Judenkongreß feierlich verkündete – (Auszug aus der 7. Sitzung):

"Sobald ein nichtjüdischer Staat es wagt, uns Juden Widerstand zu leisten, müssen wir in der Lage sein, seine Nachbarn **zum Kriege gegen ihn** zu veranlassen.... Als Mittel dazu werden wir die **öffentliche Meinung** vorschützen. Diese werden wir vorher durch die sogenannte "achte Großmacht", **die Presse** in unserem Sinne bearbeiten. Mit ganz wenig Ausnahmen, die überhaupt nicht in Frage kommen, liegt die ganze Presse der Welt in unseren Händen."

Nach einem großangelegten Plan hat in diesen Tagen der Jude die öffentliche Weltmeinung gegen Deutschland aufgehetzt. Er bedient sich dazu der **Presse**, durch die er eine ungeheure Lügenflut über die Welt ergießt. Kein Verbrechen, keine Schandtat ist ihm zu niederträchtig, er beschuldigt die **Deutschen** damit.

Der Jude lügt, in Deutschland würden Angehörige des jüdischen Volkes grausam zu Tode gefoltert.

Der Jude lügt, es würden diesen Juden die Augen ausgebrannt, die Hände abgehackt, Ohren und Nasen abgeschnitten, ja, selbst die Leichen würden noch zerstückelt.

Der Jude lügt, es würden in Deutschland selbst jüdische Frauen in grauenvoller Weise getötet und jüdische Mädchen vor den Augen ihrer Eltern vergewaltigt.

Der Jude verbreitet diese Lügen in derselben Weise und zu demselben Zwecke, wie er das auch während des Krieges getan hatte. Er will die Welt gegen Deutschland aufwiegeln.

Darüber hinaus fordert er zum

Boykott deutscher Erzeugnisse

auf. Er will damit das Elend der Arbeitslosigkeit in Deutschland noch vergrößern, er will den deutschen Export ruinieren.

Deutsche Volksgenossen!   Deutsche Volksgenossinnen!

Die Schuldigen an diesem wahnwitzigen Verbrechen, an dieser niederträchtigen Greuel- und Boykott-Hetze sind die

Juden in Deutschland

Sie haben ihre Rassegenossen im Ausland zum Kampf gegen das deutsche Volk aufgerufen. Sie haben die Lügen und Verleumdungen hinausgemeldet. Darum hat die Reichsleitung der deutschen Freiheitsbewegung beschlossen, in Abwehr der verbrecherischen Hetze

ab Samstag, den 1. April 1933 vormittags 10 Uhr

über alle jüdischen Geschäfte, Warenhäuser, Kanzleien usw.

den Boykott zu verhängen.

Dieser Boykottierung Folge zu leisten, dazu rufen wir Euch, deutsche Frauen und Männer, auf!

Kauft nichts in jüdischen Geschäften und Warenhäusern!

Geht nicht zu jüdischen Rechtsanwälten! Meidet jüdische Aerzte!

Zeigt den Juden, daß sie nicht ungestraft Deutschland in seiner Ehre herabwürdigen und beschmutzen können. Wer gegen diese Aufforderung handelt, beweist damit, daß er auf der Seite der Feinde Deutschlands steht.

Es lebe der ehrwürdige Generalfeldmarschall aus dem großen Kriege, der Reichspräsident **Paul von Hindenburg!**

Es lebe der Führer und Reichskanzler **Adolf Hitler!**

Es lebe das **Deutsche Volk** und das heilige **Deutsche Vaterland!**

Plakat Nr. 1

Druck: Max Schmidt & Söhne · München

Zentral-Komitee zur Abwehr der jüdischen Greuel- und Boykotthetze.

gez.: **Streicher.**

*The Weizmanns and friends
on the site of their future home
in Rehovot, 1934*

Towards the end of that year, Lloyd George paid a remarkable tribute to Weizmann: "Ah, yes, in my life I have met a
great many interesting people but I don't know anyone for
whom I have a greater respect than Weizmann. He is the
greatest man the Jews have thrown up in the last 1000 years.
He is a world famous figure now, and in a thousand years
from now, he will be remembered by the Jews, and he will
be the only Jew now living whose name will then be
remembered."

Weizmann pursued his rescue work at an increasing tempo
as the "intellectual forces of Jewry in Central Europe were
faced by catastrophe", in Weizmann's words. He convened
an extraordinary meeting of the Board of Governors of the
Hebrew University in April, 1933, to create opportunities
for refugees who could teach and undertake research work
there; he assumed office as Director of the Central Bureau for
the Settlement of German Jews in Palestine; he found
sanctuary for exiled Jewish scientists at the Daniel Sieff

Settlers in Rehovot in the 1930's

Research Institute in Rehovot, established by his friends, (the Marks and Sieff families of London) — "the outer shell of the building is ready and the people there are beginning with the inner outfit. Dr. Bergmann will be leaving here for Rehovot in November, and I intend to follow in two to three weeks — the laboratory will be in working order on 1 January", he wrote to a fellow scientist, late in 1933, outlining his intentions to work and live in Palestine.

"You must not think that Rehovot is merely an ivory tower on a *pis aller*", Weizmann wrote to Felix Warburg, who had resigned his position as Chairman of the Administrative Committee of the Jewish Agency, in protest against the Passfield White Paper (1930), but was still directly involved in constructive work in the Yishuv, through the Palestine Economic Corporation.

The plight of the refugees strengthened Weizmann's conviction that "We have to rely primarily on our own forces, and it is by our achievements that we shall be judged. For us, the moral basis of our cause and our faith in it remain unshaken".

Among the hundreds of individual cases of need that he concerned himself with, a few made an exceptional impression on him at that time, like the admission of personal defeat by

Zionist leaders, including Ben Zvi, Shertok, Weizmann, Arlosoroff, meet Transjordanian sheikhs in Jerusalem

Rebecca D. Sieff addresses women Zionists in London (1934) with Weizmann as guest of honour

an outstanding German Jewish scientist and friend, Fritz Haber, whose formula for the synthesis of ammonia from its elements aided Germany during the first World War, at the very time when Dr. Weizmann's work on acetone was invaluable to England.

Exiled from Germany in 1933, Prof. Haber was a broken man, when he said to Weizmann, speaking to him in Zermatt, Switzerland: "Dr. Weizmann, I was one of the mightiest men in Germany. I was than a great army commander, more than a captain of industry. I was the founder of industries; my work was essential for the economic and military expansion of Germany. All doors were open to me... at the end of my life, I find myself a bankrupt. When I am gone and forgotten, *your* work in creating out of nothing, in a land which lacks everything... will stand, a shining monument in the long history of our people".

"I have given up these last two years almost entirely to the Institute and to the German settlement work," Weizmann wrote to Dr. N. Ratnoff, in New York. He nevertheless went up once a week, while living and working in Rehovot, to attend meetings of the Jewish Agency Executive in Jerusalem. Presiding over those meetings was the leader of the Labour Movement in the *Yishuv*, David Ben Gurion.

The Daniel Sieff Institute, opened in April, 1934

Later buildings on the campus of the Weizmann Institute of Science: the Department of Physics, 1958

Ullmann Institute of Life Sciences, 1952

A view of Weizmann's "lab"

"I am attached to the workers by very strong ties",
Weizmann admitted in 1934. "I don't know anything about
socialism, but I evaluate men according to their creative
powers. When I travel through Palestine, I see everywhere
the activity of workers. This is what gives them a position
in the land and in our movement".

At that time, he came to admire the valiant efforts of
Henrietta Szold, the Founder of *Hadassah*. "At an age well
beyond that of usual retirement from public life, she has
undertaken and carried through with magnificent effective-
ness, the direction of Youth Aliyah... she is one of the most
remarkable figures in modern Jewish history."

*Henrietta Szold at the podium
at a Zionist Congress*

*Communal care
for kibbutz babies*

In the course of one of his European journeys in 1934, Weizmann renewed an acquaintance with Benito Mussolini, dictator of Italy, whom he had met shortly after *Il Duce* in 1922 had marched on Rome and seized power. At that meeting, Mussolini had said to Weizmann, "Do you know, Dr. Weizmann, not all Jews are Zionists?" Weizmann replied: "Of course I know it only too well, and not all Italians are *Fascisti*!"

At the 1934 meeting, Mussolini volunteered his help in arranging a partition of Palestine and promising a Jewish State. Weizmann was unimpressed. "I suggested deferring any discussion along the lines of a Jewish State until the population of Eretz Israel has reached half a million". Mussolini presented Weizmann with a signed photograph of himself!

Signed portrait of Mussolini given to Weizmann (note year 1934 designated as year XII, referring to the Fascist advent)

Palestine was comparatively quiet during the years of Weizmann's demission from office as President of the World Zionist Organisation, due in no small measure to the firm and fair handling by the High Commissioner, Sir Arthur Wauchope, who in 1931 after Sir John Chancellor's unimpressive term in office had succeeded him.

The future town of Holon

Setting up a new kibbutz

"Tower and stockade" — founding a new kibbutz

On 1 January, 1935, Weizmann wrote to Sir Arthur Wauchope from Rehovot: "Your acceptance of a further term of office in this country fulfils in the happiest way my own hopes for a brighter opening of the New Year. I hope and believe you will find almost as much satisfaction in continuing to live in and- work for Palestine, as we here feel in having you at the helm. For myself, I need not tell you how happy I am to think I am to have the pleasure and privilege of working with you here in years to come".

Throughout the first half of that year, in Weizmann's own words "pressure was brought to bear from quite unexpected quarters" to stand once more for the Presidency of the World Zionist Organisation, although he was not a member of the Zionist Executive.

Early in September, Weizmann wrote to his colleague in Rehovot, Dr. E.D. Bergmann, from London: "I am afraid you will feel a little disappointed at my having accepted the Presidency of the W.Z.O., but it was Fate that really took the decision. All I can say is that my devotion and attention to Rehovot will not be diminished".

At the XIXth. Zionist Congress, which met in Lucerne, the Zionist Revisionists, who had broken away from the W.Z.O. to form their own New Zionist Organisation headed by Jabotinsky, were absent. Labour Zionists, led by Ben Gurion,

were the strongest party, and supported Weizmann's policy of restraint and development.

"Our settlement work has been achieved without firing a shot; we did not build our home on other people's backs. We have revived and recultivated swampy, sandy and malaria-infested districts. And it is not true — no, it is not true that we have uprooted the Arabs. We have not uprooted them; we have shown them the way to a better life, and we will continue to do this, until they will understand that we

Gymnastic display by Zionist youth
at Zionist Congress in Lucerne, 1935

have a common interest in reviving the Middle East and that this task can be achieved only on the basis of a strong Jewish Palestine. However hard, however perilous and stony the way may be, we shall go along this road".

In those words, Weizmann presented his programme to the Zionist movement and the world.

Weizmann returned to office at a time when the shadows were closing in on the Jewish people, on Europe and the world. In Germany, Hitler's *Reichstag* had passed the Nuremberg Laws, defining the status of the Jew in Germany as a non-person, and presaging the subsequent anti-Jewish decrees of the Third Reich. In Spain, the bitter civil war had begun, wreaking its path of physical destruction and polarising political attitudes among the world's statesmen, intellectuals and even masses. With an attack on Abyssinia, Mussolini embarked on a programme of military adventurism and overt racialism. The democracies appeased the aggressors with a policy of non-intervention. In Soviet Russia, Stalin pursued a policy of ruthless purges.

And in Palestine, the Grand Mufti of Jerusalem instigated a series of riots which amounted to 'an Arab Revolt'.

Weizmann's attitude was hardening. On 2 February, 1936, he wrote to the American Zionist leader, Rabbi Stephen Wise: "You know that politically I am a moderate man, but I am

Weizmann at opening of the Levant Fair, Tel Aviv

*Riots break out
in Old City of Jerusalem*

biding my time. I think the moment is come now for a serious
attempt towards some sort of organisation which may be
less than a State, but certainly more than what the Jewish
Agency is now". And some months after the riots, before
the arrival of the Peel Commission sent by the British Government to investigate the murderous attacks by Arabs upon
Jews and the violent assaults by Arabs upon the British
military and police, Weizmann wrote to Moshe Shertok
(Sharett), a member of the Jewish Agency Executive in
Palestine: "I feel that somebody on behalf of the Jews may
have to say (possibly in next Friday's debate in the House of
Commons) that the Jews are quite prepared to defend their
own settlements, if they are only given the chance to do so,
and that we are pressing for the formation of a militia defence
force..."

Two of "the Six Million"

The Royal (Peel) Commission sat from November, 1936 to January, 1937. It heard some 120 witnesses. Its 400 page Report, published in July, 1937 is considered to be masterly in its grasp of the situation. Weizmann's key evidence before it ranged over every aspect of the Jewish National Home, its origins, aspirations and historic validity.

He said, *inter alia*. "The Jewish problem as it presents itself today can be expressed in one word: the problem of the homelessness of a people... individual Jews and individual groups of Jews may have homes and sometimes very comfortable homes but... everything to the east of the Rhine is today in a position, politically and economically which may be described — and I am not given, I think, to exaggeration — as something that is neither life nor death... these six million Jews are condemned to live from hand to mouth, they do not know today what is going to happen tomorrow... there are six million Jews pent up in places where they are not wanted and for whom the world is divided into places where they cannot live and places into which they cannot enter...

The Peel Royal Commission in Palestine

The Peel Commission in session in Jerusalem

"The German attitude has its imitators, in France and even in England and America... and so uneasiness has spread throughout Jewry—justifiable uneasiness. Very often, we say to ouselves ...but it can never happen in England, it can never happen in France... yet only recently, on the appointment of M. Blum in France (to the Premiership), I walked through the streets of Paris and I heard the familiar cry "Down with the Jews, death to the Jews!". It may be only talk but it is not pleasant. It makes one uneasy.

"There should be one place in the world, in God's wide world, where we could live and express ourselves in accordance with our character and make our contribution to the civilised world in our own way and through our own channels... this steadfastness which has preserved the Jew is primarily due to some physiological or psychological attachment to Palestine. We have never forgotten it, nor given it up. During the nineteen centuries which have passed since the destruction of Palestine as a Jewish political entity, there was not a single century in which the Jews did not attempt to come back — when the material props of the Jewish Commonwealth were destroyed, the Jews carried Palestine in their hearts and in their heads wherever they went — I think the Balfour Declaration is but the final link in the chain of attempts made by the British people to help us to come back to Palestine...

Flag Day in Tel Aviv

"It is a fallacy to think that what has been built up in Palestine has been built by the rich Jews ...I was instrumental in raising a great part of the public funds which have been sunk in this country. Between 1900 and the present day, I have been to America 11 times, once to South Africa, innumerable times in various parts of Europe and I know my clientele, so to speak. They are the poor and the middle class... a people which for centuries had been divorced from agricultural pursuits... from pioneering... after 15 years we stand before an achievement which I think one can look on with a certain amount of respect, and on which we look with a certain amount of pride..."

Weizmann and Ben Gurion, after giving their evidence to the Peel Commission

Ussishkin and Weizmann
at the Levant Fair

At the XXth. Zionist Congress, which took place in Zurich shortly after the publication of the Peel Report, Weizmann expressed opposition to the Commission's recommendation that Palestine be partitioned, but proposed that the Zionist movement should negotiate with the British Government to discover the precise terms for the proposed establishment of a Jewish State.

Anticipating the recommendation of the Peel Commission, Weizmann, emerging from a session of the Commission in Jerusalem in December, 1936, had told a colleague: "A Jewish State, the idea of Jewish independence in Palestine, is such a lofty thing that it ought to be treated like the Ineffable Name, which is never pronounced in vain."

Weizmann's name was freely used to canvass support among British leaders for a proposal that the Jewish State in Palestine should be established as a seventh Dominion of the

Weizmann surrounded by
the Daniel Sieff Institute staff

Arturo Toscanini (r.), in Palestine for Inaugural Concert by Palestine
Philharmonic Orchestra, founded by Bronislaw Huberman (l.), visits
the Daniel Sieff Research Institute, 1936

The Weizmanns and Moshe Shertok
on a visit to Hanita,
on the Lebanese border

British Commonwealth. Replying to a letter from Lord
Melchett, the principal Anglo-Jewish sponsor of the scheme,
Lord Tweedsmuir (formerly the novelist, John Buchan),
Governor-General of Canada and a former chairman of the
British parliamentary pro-Palestine Committee, wrote on 30
November, 1937: "Your letter has given me the first ray of
light. I have no comment to make, but if you and Weizmann
think the scheme practicable it certainly has my assent".
Weizmann, however, declined to be inveigled by enthusiasts
for the "seventh Dominion" idea into any diversion from the
main issue — a Jewish State.

With a mandate from the Zionist Congress, Weizmann
proceeded to negotiate partition, and its *sine qua non*, a Jewish
State with fraternal ties with Britain. The British, however,
were retracting from partition. Malcolm MacDonald, was
Minister for the Colonies and the Dominions. Some seven
years earlier, he had been the most effective liaison between
his father, Ramsay MacDonald, the first British Labour
Prime Minister and Weizmann, in repairing the broken
bridges between the Government and the Jewish Agency
over the Passfield White Paper.

"He has our complete confidence and if you will allow me
to say so, our most sincere affection," Weizmann had written
to Ramsay MacDonald in November, 1930. But now Malcolm
MacDonald was pursuing a devious course. With Europe
drifting to war and Italy an active member of the anti-
Comintern Pact, the British Government was ready to traduce
the Balfour Declaration and to alter the terms of their Mandate.

Weizmann appealed to Smuts, the last surviving member of the British War Cabinet which had formulated the policy of supporting a Jewish National Home in Palestine. Smuts was one of many outstanding voices of protest against the "British betrayal", as Weizmann called it. He was joined in his protest by Winston Churchill.

Churchill, out of office since 1929, had come to know Dr. Weizmann on an intimate level. Their relationship, at times, was quite informal. For instance, in an exchange of opinions on the recommendations of the Peel Commission, when discussing the tactics to be employed by the Parliamentary opponents of British policy in Palestine, Churchill deferred to Weizmann's views, saying "Dr. Weizmann, in this matter, you are the boss!".

In a speech in the House of Commons on 23 May, 1939, Churchill castigated the MacDonald White Paper as "a violation of the pledge . . . the abandonment of the Balfour Declaration, the end of the vision, of the hope, of the dream . . . what sort of a National Home is offered to the Jews of the world, when we are asked to declare that in five years time, the door of that Home is to be shut and barred?"

In a letter to the London 'Times', in January, 1939, Weizmann stated, "Jewish settlement in Palestine has succeeded because every furrow ploughed, every tree planted, is sanctified into an act of national redemption".

Weizmann explained to Lord Tweedsmuir why he felt frustrated in his dealings with the British Government: "I find myself dealing with 'Pharoahs' who 'know not Joseph'... their standards and their outlook differ widely from those which animated Balfour... Everything seems to be overlaid with a kind of surrealism... theirs is a doctrine of temporary. expediency, opportunism..."

Leon Blum, a former French Premier, had warned Weizmann, in February, 1939: "There is a wild hunger for physical safety which paralyses the power of thought. People are ready to buy the illusion of security at any price, hoping against hope that something will happen to save their

Discussing plans for the Hebrew University with members of the Board of Governors, London, 1938

countries from invasion". Weizmann agreed. "Halifax (British Foreign Secretary), Chamberlain (British Prime Minister) and Malcolm MacDonald (Colonial Secretary) have been vitiated from the outset by this frightful mood of frustration and panic. They are determined to placate the Arabs just as they are placating Hitler", he wrote.

The British convened a tripartite conference in London — the 'Round Table Conference'. It was a fiasco. The Arabs refused even to enter St. James's Palace, where it took place, through the same door as the Jewish delegation, led by Weizmann.

Weizmann told the British representatives: "You cannot stop an organic growth; you cannot stop a plant from growing: you cannot stop the sun from turning round; it is a natural process. Only Joshua succeeded in doing it, and I am afraid I cannot attempt it."

Malcolm MacDonald

Weizmann, Ben Gurion and Shertok
in London for the Round Table Conference

The Conference was marked by a *contretemps* in the dispatch of a letter addressed to Weizmann, but apparently meant only for the eyes of the Arab delegation. The letter spelt out the outline of the White Paper of 1939 — an Arab State of Palestine in five years — limited Jewish immigration, until the Arab State was established and none thereafter without Arab consent. MacDonald maintained that the letter was in fact merely a draft minute, not intended for circulation at all. MacDonald was now even more suspect in Jewish eyes. Among his colleagues, Weizmann persisted in advocating a course of action which would not entail a final break in relations with the Government.

To Weizmann, it was not merely the framework of the British proposals which were unacceptable, but their implications. "If we cannot get an appreciable number of Jews into Palestine or acquire land there, further discussion would become useless", he told his Zionist colleagues.

The Jewish representatives...

...and the Arab representatives

Weizmann appealed to Smuts to come to England. He told MacDonald bluntly that "everything had been pre-judged, that his strategic arguments were bunk, that he had betrayed them". The Conference ended in disarray. Weizmann terminated the proceedings for the Jewish delegation, by telling them that: "All that was happening was an episode, one more turn in the ups and downs that we have known. We had wonderful hopes and these have been partly shattered. We have waited for thousands of years, and we will plod along for another five years".

In spite of an appeal by Weizmann, to Chamberlain, the British Prime Minister, the White Paper was published in May. "The Balfour Declaration", according to Weizmann "has been annulled".

The XXIst. Zionist Congress, held in Geneva in late August, 1939, was the shortest on record.

"We met under the shadow of the White Paper, which threatened the destruction of the National Home", Weizmann recalled.

In the service of science

*Featherstone Buildings, Holborn, London,
the elegant 18th century building
where Weizmann had a laboratory*

*The last Zionist Congress
held before the war.
Geneva, 1939*

In his inaugural address, he stated: "In this solemn hour, I am reluctantly compelled to say that the British Government has gone back on its promises. It is not easy for me — above all for me — to have to say it... an international obligation to the Jews in regard to a sacred land, undertaken before the whole civilised world, cannot be unilaterally destroyed... the British Government has taken upon itself to try to bring to a standstill the great historic process of the return of Israel and the rebuilding of Palestine, which began long before the country came under British rule... the Government may itself be the victim of an illusion, the illusion that you can counter force by further force, directed not against the aggressors but against the victims... We must and shall defend our lives, our rights, our work, with all the strength at our disposal... Whatever may happen today, tomorrow, or in the near future, the work our pioneers have achieved will live and grow, and remain a permanent source of strength and courage to this and future generations".

His closing address, delivered after Congress had heard the news of the Ribbentrop-Molotov Pact between Germany and Russia was prophetic: "There is darkness around us... if, as I hope, we are spared in life and our work continues, who knows — perhaps a new light will shine upon us from the thick, bleak gloom... the remnant shall work on, fight on, live on until the dawn of better days. Towards that dawn, I greet you. May we meet again in peace".

*At the Congress on hearing the news of
the signing of the Molotov-Ribbentrop Pact*

Towards The State

Benjamin Weizmann in uniform

Michael Weizmann in uniform

Ten days later, Hitler invaded Poland. The Second World War had begun. Just as Weizmann had predicted, "the Jewish people would survive through its remnants".

The two Weizmann sons, Benjamin and Michael, enlisted immediately on the outbreak of the war, Benjie joining an artillery battalion, Michael the Royal Air Force.

For the first eight months of the war, Winston Churchill was once again First Lord of the Admiralty, as he had been for a period during the First World War, during which time he had instructed Weizmann to make thirty thousand tons of acetone for the guns of the Royal Navy.

Weizmann, restless and uncertain what role he could play in this phase of the war — it was the lull before the storm in Western Europe, the period known as 'The Phony War' — made an exploratory visit to the United States.

On 17 December, 1939, before flying to New York, "the first of a number of hazardous wartime trans-Atlantic crossings," as Vera Weizmann recalled them, Weizmann called on Churchill. "We talked of certain land legislation, very unfavourable to us, which was being proposed for Palestine, and it was particularly encouraging to find him, at such a time, mindful of us and our problems".

"You have stood at the cradle of the enterprise", Weizmann reminded Churchill, "I hope you will see it through... after the war, we want to build up a State of three or four million Jews". Churchill replied positively, "Yes, indeed, I quite agree with that!"

Congratulating Lord Lothian, (Sir Philip Kerr) on his appointment as British Ambassador to Washington, shortly after the outbreak of the war, he had written to him: "... the Jews of America are taking an outstanding part in our activities. As you know, they had an important share in the developments and negotiations which preceded the Balfour Declaration and they have ever since remained prominent in our ranks both in the sphere of diplomatic effort and of financial assistance... it is not surprising, therefore, that American Jews should be up in arms against the prospect of their efforts being handed over to the tender mercies of the Mufti and his associates. We have here in Palestine a good many American pioneers in our agricultural settlements, young men and women who came not because of any persecution, but essentially because they saw in the work of national redemption, the promise of a more significant life. The American Jews have also taken a very distinguished part in the building up of our great institutions of learning. The Hebrew University in Jerusalem and the Medical School about to be inaugurated have been established essentially through American endeavour. No community has a more significant stake in the new Palestine than American Jewry".

Weizmann signs World Fair register 1939, in presence of Fair President Grover Whalen

*1940 Protest meeting in Tel Aviv
against new Land Regulations
promulgated by the Palestine British Government*

In Hollywood with singing stars Nelson Eddy and Jeannette MacDonald and movie mogul Louis B. Mayer

Weizmann was frustrated by his first wartime stay in the United States. He found Americans "out of touch with the realities of the European situation".

He was 65 years-old, but he was still anxious to serve the Allied war effort. Appointed Honorary Chemical Adviser to the Ministry of Supply, he worked in an improvised laboratory set up in Grosvenor Mews with a small group of chemists, to find a process to crack oil. The Weizmanns moved out of Kensington, sold their house, and took up temporary residence in the Dorchester Hotel, close to the laboratory.

In a letter to Meyer Weisgal in New York, written in May, 1940, at the height of the Nazi *blitzkrieg*, Weizmann wrote: "...the whole responsibility henceforth falls on America due to the terrible, indisputable fact that European Jewry, with very few exceptions, has been practically blotted out. The foundations of everything in which we believe are rocking... I am confident that the onslaught of the German hordes will be stopped in the end; but when, and at what cost, no one can say".

He repeated that theme when he re-visited America: "Every conceivable effort of American Jewry should be devoted towards helping the Allies in this struggle, which is our struggle. If the battle here should be lost, there will be no hope for you, and very little for America as a whole".

After the fall of France, when the British Isles stood alone to face the fury of the Germans, Weizmann wrote to A.K. Epstein, a Zionist colleague, in Chicago: "As regards ourselves, we shall go on fighting, and we are confident of victory. If we survive the storm, we shall have to adapt ourselves to the new conditions then to be created. Whether we who have carried the Movement thus far along its course, happen to survive or not is perhaps irrelevant... *Everything* is at stake today and 3000 miles of water will not save American Jewry or America itself, if they refuse to take the right decisions now".

Grosvenor Mews where Weizmann
set up his wartime laboratory

Special wartime service in a London synagogue

Chaim and Vera Weizmann were in embattled London, when the *Luftwaffe* conducted it's nightly bombing raids. He was working in his Hyde Park laboratory — "the size of a postage stamp" — and she was assigned scrutineering work by Scotland Yard, on behalf of German refugees.

Weizmann and the leadership of the *Yishuv* continued to exchange views, in a situation in which the "Battle of Britain" was the immediate crisis, but a German threat to the Middle East, a probable contingency in the Spring.

A few days after the massive German bombing raid on London on the night of 29, December, 1940, Weizmann wrote to Shertok in Jerusalem: "The days are painfully short; the dark nights are long. Physical amenities do not improve as time goes on. We in the office are only a handful, and somewhat in the nature of a polar expedition. Great care is needed in order to avoid getting on one another's nerves, while having to battle constantly against the difficulties in an atmosphere of hideous destruction. Although we all face life with quite a good deal of courage, subconsciously one suffers from the raids, and from feeling and seeing the tears and misery of others. At the same time, I would be unfair if I omitted to tell you that it is an elevating, a grandiose spectacle to see this small country facing a ruthless enemy single-handed under the leadership of a man who is growing in stature day by day — and who, I am happy to say is consistently friendly to us."

The imminent threat to Palestine strengthened the case for a Jewish Army. Towards the end of 1940, Weizmann was led to believe by the highest British authorities that official sanction would be given to the idea. Accordingly, he wrote to Shertok: "The (British) Government has at last agreed to the formation of a Jewish Army on the same basis, and I believe with the same status, as the Czech or Polish Army. Its size to begin with is to be about 10,000 assuming that 4,000 would come from Palestine and another 6,000 from the rest of the world, America in particular... Orde Wingate has gone to Egypt as a staff officer to Wavell... I have impressed upon Orde repeatedly; he must try and work in with Wavell, just as Lawrence did with Allenby..." An optimistic note from his son, Michael, confirms the extent to which Weizmann believed that the British agreement on the Jewish Army would be implemented quickly: "I am so glad you've got the Jewish Army at last. Perhaps I shall get a job there in connection with the Air Force!"

Orde Wingate (r.) and a fellow officer

To Weizmann from Prime Minister Winston Churchill

In a note to Brendan Bracken M.P. who was to become British Information Minister, with whom he was on intimate terms, Weizmann referred to proposals he had submitted to the Prime Minister for "Jewish Desert Units", and, describing these as "the best beginning for the Jewish fighting force", requested that "it be commanded by Wingate. He knows our people, was highly successful in dealing with them, and has our complete confidence".

However, neither Churchill's assurances, nor the intervention of influential men like Smuts were effective against the stolid resistance from the British Foreign Office to the idea of recruiting Jews in Palestine. Only towards the end of the war, was action taken to implement promises made to Weizmann, who admitted that he found it very difficult to explain to American Jewry the British tactics of procrastination, when speaking to them in 1941 and 1942.

On the eve of their departure from London for New York in February, 1942, tragedy struck the Weizmanns. Michael Weizmann was posted missing, off the coast of France.

"Perhaps Michael had come down safely after all; perhaps he was a prisoner in the hands of the Germans, and we would not hear of it for a long time because he would not give his real name; perhaps, then, some day we would hear from him

The Weizmanns arrive in America

Travelling in America

again. It was a vain hope that pursued us for years, and it died completely only with the ending of the war", Weizmann wrote.

The attack on Pearl Harbour in December 1941 brought the United States into the war. President Roosevelt asked for Weizmann's presence in the United States, to work there on the problem of producing synthetic rubber. The American Ambassador in London advised Weizmann to devote himself once again, almost entirely to chemistry — "I would thus serve best both the Allied Powers and the Zionist cause... actually, I devoted my time about equally between science and Zionism".

In the words of a close observer of the scene in wartime Washington, Isaiah Berlin; "Weizmann stuck to his guns; not to alienate Churchill and the pro-Zionists in the British Cabinet; to talk and to talk again to responsible people, 'that is how the Balfour Declaration had been secured — marches, petitions, resolutions, advertisements in the press with signatures of prominent persons, philippics — all this might impress the Jews, it would not succeed in moving Washington' Weizmann believed".

Already in September, 1940, Weizmann had drawn up a brief note for the British Ministry of Supply on the inadequacy of U.S. production of high-octane fuel for the joint requirements of the U.S. and Britain. "In order to keep in the air an offensive Air Force," Weizmann pointed out, "provision should be made at once for the opening up of new sources of high-octane fuel...alternative sources can be found...from materials available within the British Empire, e.g., in Canada, India, the West Indies and other places", after stating that "the world's annual production of crude oil may be estimated at some 300,000,000 tons, of which the U.S. produces some 100,000,000 tons", annually. Weizmann contended later that "Palestine could be made a centre of the new scientific development which would get the world out of the conflict arising from the monopolistic position of oil".

In his Rehovot laboratory

Franklin Delano Roosevelt

Jan Christiaan Smuts

*Weizmann, before addressing a mass meeting in Cleveland,
with his wife and Abba Hillel Silver*

Weizmann was working with a special committee under the chairmanship of Bernard Baruch, to find radical solutions to the critical shortages of rubber and aviation fuel. He was introducing a new concept in the exploitation of the world's natural resources, the concept of "Chemurgy". He submitted a paper to the British Government in which he stated: "There is a definite possibility that the feasibility of such a scheme will be tested first in Palestine, where conditions for the realisation of such a large-scale industrial project are favourable".

While Weizmann was pursuing his diplomatic campaign in Washington, and keeping up the pressure on the British Government, two Zionist leaders, Abba Hillel Silver and David Ben Gurion were restive about Weizmann's strategy and tactics, which Silver argued was out of touch with American Jewry's temper, and which Ben Gurion contended was autocratic towards his colleagues, in the *Yishuv*, and conciliatory towards the British.

Weizmann made the first clear and open declaration of the Zionist demand for, a Jewish 'Commonwealth' in Palestine after the war, in a crucial article which he wrote in October, 1941, and which appeared for the first time in the influential American journal, "Foreign Affairs": "It is for the democracies to proclaim the justice of the Jewish claim to their own commonwealth in Palestine".

Abba Hillel Silver
and Weizmann in Chicago

The Biltmore Conference, New York, 1942.
Weizmann, Ben Gurion
and the majority of the American Zionist leaders
are grouped at the top table

This theme was taken up at a conference convened in the Biltmore Hotel, New York, in May, 1942, at Dr. Weizmann's behest to hammer out a combined platform for the Zionist forces in the United States.

In consultation with Weizmann, the 'Biltmore Programme' was drawn up, denouncing the 1939 White Paper, demanding the implementation of the Balfour Declaration, and authorising the Jewish Agency "to direct and regulate immigration into Palestine, and to develop the agricultural and industrial possibilities and the natural resources of the country".

Ben Gurion, challenged Weizmann's leadership, sharply castigated him for various sins of omission and commission, particularly with regard to the formation of the Jewish Army, and initiated a bitter personal feud. Weizmann, unable to

Weizmann and Stephen Wise
at the Biltmore Conference

The first stage...

the second...

and the third...

Bernard Baruch

travel to Palestine, composed a letter to the Palestine Executive of the Jewish Agency, in which he denied the accusations ... "incorrect in fact and always torn out of context". Weizmann concluded his letter with a warning against Ben Gurion's "intention to re-shape the Zionist world in his own image ..."

The extent of the holocaust which overtook European Jewry in the war years was not fully known at that time, but at the Biltmore Conference, Weizmann had declared:

"In a time of worldwide calamity, when it is impossible to turn the eye in any direction without being met by the spectacle of suffering and bloodshed, it may seem invidious to award to a single people a special crown of martyrdom. But a cold evaluation — if such a thing is possible — of the horrors visited upon humanity, lifts into tragic pre-eminence one people, the Jewish, as the most consistent and helpless target of a malignant fate".

Some months later, in a *'Rosh Hashana'* message which was sent by cable from New York to the *"Zionist Review"* in London, he wrote: "In world at war, sufferings European Jewry at hands of dictatorship unexampled for coldblooded and ruthless savagery continue write terrible chapter in history mans relations with man Nazis fordoomed extinction but leaving in wake horror and misery untold stop for great masses our people Palestine still remains only light in present and only hope in future".

Weizmann and Meyer Weisgal

Weizmann among his people

At a massive "Stop Hitler Now" rally at Madison Square Garden, New York, in March, 1943 attended by some 100,000 people, under the Chairmanship of Rabbi Stephen Wise, Weizmann was the principal speaker. He declared: "When the historian of the future assembles the black record of our days, he will find two things unbelievable: first, the crime itself; second, the reaction of the world to that crime. He will sift the evidence again and again before he will be able to give credence to the fact that in the twentieth century of the Christian era, a great and cultivated nation put power into a band of assassins who transformed murder from a secret transgression into a publicly avowed government policy to be carried out with all the paraphernalia of State. He will find the monstrous story of the human slaughterhouses, the lethal chambers, the sealed trains taxing the powers of belief... He will be puzzled by the apathy of the civilised world in the face of this immense, systematic carnage of human beings whose sole guilt was membership in the people which gave the commandments of moral law to mankind... the world can no longer plead that the ghastly facts are unknown or unconfirmed... let the gates of Palestine be opened to all who can reach the shores of the Jewish home-land..."

Jews being deported

March past of the Jewish Brigade

In July, 1943, Weizmann returned to England, still leader of the Zionist movement, but deeply disturbed by its blatant disunity. "As we have seen it with governments and peoples far more powerful than we, disunity in foreign policy spells doom for that people", he wrote in an eve of departure letter from New York, to Dr. Stephen Wise.

"It is infinitely more simple to ... indulge in high-sounding but nevertheless sterile phrases than to counsel moderation, hard work and solid achievement", he warned in that letter, recalling that he had "once remarked that he never wanted to use the phrase 'Jewish State' prematurely ... it must not be used in vain".

In 1944, with the tide of war turning, Weizmann learnt from Churchill that the Jewish Brigade could be formed, although, in a letter to Weizmann in October, 1944, the British Prime Minister indicated that authority for the flag of the Jewish Brigade to be flown in Egypt would not be granted.

At a meeting with Churchill, in November, 1944, Weizmann pressed that the Negev should be included in the Jewish State. Emphasising that "American participation in the creation of a Jewish State in Palestine is essential," Churchill accepted that the Negev would be part of that Jewish State.

On the eve of his departure for Palestine, his first visit there in five years, he was deeply shocked by the assassination in Cairo on 6 November of Lord Moyne, who was Britain's Deputy Minister of State. He wrote to Churchill: "I can hardly find words adequate to express the deep moral indignation and horror which I feel at the murder of Lord Moyne. I know that these feelings are shared by Jewry throughout the world. Whether or not the criminals prove to be Palestinian Jews, their act illumines the abyss to which terrorism leads. Political crimes of this kind are an especial abomination in that they make it possible to implicate whole communities in the guilt of a few. I can assure you that Palestine Jewry will, as its representative bodies have declared, go to the utmost limit of its power to cut out, root and branch, this evil from its midst".

In November, 1944, Weizmann turned seventy.

Vera Weizmann described the week of birthday celebrations as "a week of festivities... in which Chaim was greeted as if he were already Head of State. An armed Jewish detachment paraded before him... a reception was held in his honour in Jerusalem... visits were exchanged between us and the new High Commissioner, Lord Gort".

Meyer Weisgal recalls that "my supreme desire was to be with Weizmann on his seventieth birthday... I arrived in time, bearing two birthday gifts. The first was the book

Visiting Ein Gev

(Chaim Weizmann... Builder of The Jewish Commonwealth).
The second I could not carry with me, nor was it mine alone.
It was the Weizmann Institute of Science."

Overwhelmed by the reception given to him wherever he
went in the *Yishuv*, Weizmann was disturbed by the bitter
internal dissensions which he encountered.

In a letter to Justice Felix Frankfurter, he wrote: "This is
a country which cannot live without immigration. As soon
as immigration stops, energies are diverted to fruitless, futile
discussions and political fermentation. The people begin to
stew in their own juice, they become introspective, isolated
and provincial... I am very happy to say that my visit to
Palestine so far as I am able to judge, has had a sobering
effect on the Jewish community... I am more than gratified
by the fine impression that the new High Commissioner
(Lord Gort) has made on the country... in the short weeks
he has been here, he has succeeded in lifting somewhat the
mood of the people"...

*The High Commissioner, Viscount Gort,
V.C., being greeted by the children
and settlers of Gush Etzion, 1944*

Weizmann addressing volunteers of the Jewish Brigade

Laying the cornerstone for
the Weizmann Institute of Science, June 1946

As a birthday tribute, a group of friends in England and the United States had launched a project to establish the Weizmann Institute of Science in Rehovot, with the Daniel Sieff Research Institute as its nucleus.

At the ceremony to lay the foundation stone, Weizmann's scientific colleague, Dr. E. D. Bergmann, who had been close to him for some thirteen years, declared: "We, the small group of young and unknown Jewish scientists gathered around Weizmann, are grateful to him not only because he has given us the possibility of constructive work for our great cause, but also for the example he has set us... he has shown us the way to find that peace which only the union of character and purpose can give, and without which there can be no salvation for humanity and no redemption for the Jewish people".

Weizmann toured Palestine and was thrilled by what he saw, the evidence of steady progress despite the ever-present fear of invasion, the steadfastness to the ideals of growth and ingathering, despite the restrictions imposed by the British White Paper.

The finished building

*Touring the settlements,
accompanied by Meyer Weisgal*

Inspecting volunteers

Crossing the Kinneret

*A moment's silence at the grave
of Labour Zionist ideologist
Berl Katznelson*

The Weizmanns and E.D. Bergmann

In May, 1945, after "V E Day", with the war in Europe won, Weizmann wrote to Churchill: "This is the hour to eliminate the White Paper, to open the doors of Palestine and to proclaim the Jewish State".

Two months later, Churchill was no longer in office. Bevin, the British Foreign Secretary, refused to withdraw the White Paper. In December, Weizmann turned to President Truman, who had succeeded Roosevelt in the White House, for American support for "a Jewish democratic Commonwealth, giving shelter, sustenance and peace to Jews and Arabs alike".

Bevin had appointed Labour MP., Richard Crossman to be one of six members of the English team on the Anglo-American Inquiry Commission he had sent out to Palestine at the beginning of 1946.

In his diary on 6 March, Crossman noted: "Today we had Weizmann who looks like a weary and more humane version of Lenin, very tired, very ill. He spoke for two hours with a magnificent mixture of passion and scientific detachment...

The Anglo-American Commission
on arrival in Jerusalem, 1946

Weizmann with Eleanor Roosevelt

He is the first witness who has frankly and openly admitted that the issue is not between right and wrong but between the greater and the lesser injustice. Weizmann's extraordinary hold on Britain depends entirely on an integrity which refuses to say 'I know' when he does not know..."

The report to that Commission, published on 1 May, 1946, pleased neither the British, nor the Jews, nor the Arabs. As far as Jewish action was concerned, the initiative in Palestine had been taken out of Weizmann's hands.

The summer of 1946 saw a direct confrontation between the Jews of the *Yishuv* and the British authorities. Weizmann, ill in London at the time, did his best to moderate the situation, and succeeding in persuading the British Government to arrange for the release of Zionist and *Yishuv* leaders interned in Ramle, and for the return of the Jewish Agency Building, in Jerusalem.

Ben Gurion, in a letter to Weizmann, writing from Paris on 28 October, 1946, described Weizmann thus: "You remain for me the elect of Jewish history, representing beyond compare, the suffering and the glory of the Jews... We are the generation which comes after you, and which has been tried, perhaps, by a crueller fate..."

Weizmann with Zionist colleagues
Nicolai Kirschner (S.A.)
and Louis Lipsky (U.S.A.)
in London, 1946

The XXIInd Zionist Congress opened in Basel on 9 December. Weizmann, seventy-two years old, his eye-sight and his general health impaired, his policy seemingly in ruins, dominated that Congress. In his inaugural address he said: "The shadow of tragic bereavement is upon us tonight... We feared too little and we hoped too much. We under-estimated the bestiality of the enemy; we over-estimated the humanity, the wisdom, the sense of justice of our friends... it was the tragic destiny of our young generation to see their kinsmen brutally murdered in Europe while they stood by helpless and impotent. They were prevented from receiving the few survivors whom Providence had spared... each people must apply its own standards to its conduct and we are left with the task of weighing our actions in the scales of Jewish tradition. Nor must our judgment be dazzled by the glare of selfconscious heroism. Masada, for all its heroism, was a disaster in our history... the eleven new settlements just established in the Negev have, in my deepest conviction, a far greater weight than a hundred speeches about resistance."

Heckled beyond endurance, Weizmann turned on his tormentors, saying: "somebody has called me a demagogue — I — a demagogue! I, who have borne all the ills and travails of this Movement. The person who flung that word in my face ought to know that in every house and stable in Nahalal, in every little workshop in Tel Aviv or Haifa, there is a drop of my blood..."

His concluding peroration, virtually a valedictory address, was the summation of his whole philosophy.

"I warn you against bogus palliatives, against short cuts, against false prophets, against facile generations, against distortions of historic facts... If you think you are bringing the redemption nearer by un-Jewish methods, if you have lost faith in hard work and better days, then you are committing idolatry, and endangering what we have built. Would that I had a tongue of flame, the strength of prophets, to warn you against the paths of Babylon and Egypt. Zion shall be redeemed in righteousness, and not by any other means... Masada, for all its heroism, was a disaster in our history. It is not our purpose or our right to plunge to destruction in order to bequeath a legend of martyrdom to posterity. Zionism was to mark the end of our glorious deaths and the beginning of a new path, leading to life. Against the heroics of suicidal violence, I urge the courage of endurance, the heroism of human restraint", he declared.

"Black Saturday," 29 June 1946 – Leaders of the Jewish Agency imprisoned in Latrun. (l. to r.) David Remez, Moshe Shertok, Yitzhak Gruenbaum, Bernard (Dov) Joseph, A. Shenkar, David Hacohen, Chaim Halperin

Press Conference during UNSCOP sessions

Mines on the Tel Aviv seashore

Fighting breaks out in Jerusalem

A convoy in the beleag[...]
city of Jerusalem, 194[...]

Weizmann, flanked by Abba Eban,
giving evidence to UNSCOP

The Congress listened to Weizmann, but rejected his programme. "For the second time in two decades, the Zionist movement had first dismissed Weizmann, then followed his advice", in the words of Abba Eban, former Israel Foreign Minister, who throughout the 1940's was a close associate of Weizmann.

Out of office, Weizmann was nevertheless considered a key witness when the United Nations Special Committee on Palestine took evidence late in 1947. On 1, October, addressing *UNSCOP* in New York, Weizmann said: "The character of our movement as a genuine effort at national liberation and society building cannot be obscured by slanders... I will not discuss whether it is a good or a bad fortune to be a minority in an Arab state. I would leave the Jews of Iraq, of Yemen and Tripoli — and the Christian Assyrians of Iraq to pronounce upon that... a world which does not hear us in this moment of our agony would be deaf to the voice of justice and human feeling which must be raised loud and clear if the moral foundations of our society are to survive".

Weizmann receives members of UNSCOP in Rehovot

One of the congratulatory letters Weizmann received on his birthday gave him special satisfaction, tinged with sorrow. It came from Joel Brand, the Hungarian Jew whose part in a bold attempt to rescue the Jews of Hungary in an exchange for trucks, in May 1944, had proved abortive. Brand had reached Palestine from Turkey, and writing in Tel Aviv, said: "We all wish you to lead us for many more years and see with your own eyes the realisation of a real Eretz Israel... permit me to express the thanks of Hungarian Jewry for your help and big efforts undertaken by you towards their rescue, as far as it was possible. We know well that you are still doing whatever it is in your power and would ask you not to relax your efforts..."

Under the protectio
of the Jewish flag

E.D. Bergmann with
the Weizmanns on their travels

*Weizmann talking to Lillie Shultz
and Meyer Weisgal at Lake Success, 1947*

In November, the General Assembly of the United Nations debated the partition of Palestine. Britain had already given notice of its intention to lay down the Mandate and to quit the region.

On 27 November, Weizmann wrote a letter to President Truman, thanking him for a private audience the President had given him in the White House: "Fears are also expressed that our project in Palestine may in some way be used as a channel for the infiltration of Communist ideas in the Middle East. Nothing is further from the truth. An educated peasantry and a skilled industrial class living on high standards will never accept Communism. The danger lies amongst illiterate and impoverished communities bearing no resemblance to our own".

*Weizmann, supported by his wife,
and Eban on their way to
UNSCOP hearing, June 1947*

*Weizmann presenting the case for a Jewish State
at the U.N. in October 1947*

In that same week, Weizmann had rallied support for the
UNSCOP partition plan from world leaders whose respect,
gained when he was in office, had enhanced, now that he was
world Jewry's elder statesman.

At the United Nations, he scorned Jamal el-Husseini's asser-
tion that "the Jews of today were in fact Tartars, unconnected
with Palestine".

"I have been told that I am a Tartar, a Khazar, a German,
an Englishman, anything but a Jew," he said. "All I know is
that all my life, I lived like a Jew, suffered like a Jew, and am
still bearing the sufferings of my people".

On 29 November, 1947, the General Assembly of the United Nations approved the separation of Palestine into separate States, Jewish and Arab.

At a mass rally of Jews in New York that night, Weizmann's appearance led to scenes of near pandemonium. He was lifted from the car which the police had escorted to the St. Nicholas Arena, onto the shoulders of the jubilant throng, and carried into the hall. He wept, as the crowds sang *"Hatikvah",* the anthem of the renascent Jewish people, soon to be the anthem of the reborn Jewish State.

Shertok congratulating Weizmann on 29 November 1947

...ERS OF THE COOPERATIVE JEWISH STATE

...VEMBER 29, 1947

A few hours after the
guests at 24th annual

United Nations decision to establish the Jewish State, 11,000 delegates and
on of National Committee for Labor Palestine launched $7,500,000 drive for
Histadrut.

...Tel Aviv, November 29, 1947

Weizmann, Eddie Jacobson and wife

The U.N. decision led to a new outbreak of violence in Palestine. Weizmann's experience, wisdom and charisma were needed to defend the Jewish case in the forum of the nations of the world and in the corridors of power in Washington. Truman, unwilling to grant Weizmann another audience at the critical hour, was persuaded by an old friend, Eddie Jacobson to give Weizmann another hearing: "I have never met the man who has been my hero all my life but I have studied his past just as you have studied (President) Jackson's" Jacobson wrote to Truman in March, 1948, "He is the greatest Jew alive, perhaps the greatest Jew who ever lived. You yourself have told me that he is a great statesman and a fine gentleman... I am talking about Chaim Weizmann. He is an old man and a very sick man. He has travelled thousands of miles to see you and now you are putting off seeing him. That isn't like you!"

President Truman greeting
"The Old Doctor" in Washington

227

Truman, in his Memoirs, wrote:

"Dr. Weizmann came on March 18 and we talked for almost three-quarters of an hour. He talked about the possibilities of development in Palestine, about the scientific work that he and his assistants had done that someday would be translated into industrial activity in the Jewish State he envisaged. He spoke of the need for land if the future immigrants were to be cared for, and he impressed on me the importance of the Negev area in the south to any future Jewish State. Dr. Weizmann was a man of remarkable achievements and personality. His life been dedicated to two ideals, that of science and that of the Zionist movement. He was past seventy now, and in ill-health. He had known many disappointments and had grown patient and wise in them."

air House, Washington, D.C., where Dr. Weizmann
as the guest of President Truman

Interviewed by the Press,
aboard the s.s. Queen Mary

The Jewish Agency was poised for the fateful step, the declaration of the State of Israel. Timing was important. As the moment for decision drew nearer, Weizmann was in the United States, at the request of the Zionist leadership, lobbying at UNO, and on hand to explain the Jewish stance to Presidents, and Governments. *"Vos warten zey, die idioten!"* ("What are they waiting for, the idiots!") — Weizmann instructed Weisgal to inform Ben Gurion, only hours before the Declaration of Independence, on 15 May, 1948.

A cable was signed by David Ben Gurion, Golda Meyerson (Meir), David Remez and Eliezer Kaplan, on behalf of the Jewish Provisional Government and sent to Weizmann, prior to the solemn reading of the Declaration and the affixing of signatures to it but no provision was made to have Weizmann's signature on the historic document. The text of the cable was: "On the occasion of the establishment of the Jewish State, we send our greetings to you, who have done more than any living man towards its creation. Your stand and help have strengthened all of us. We look forward to the day when we shall greet you at the head of the State, established in peace".

Golda Meir was one of the signatories who cabled urging Weizmann to accept the Presidency

Prime Minister and Preside... Ben Gurion and Weizm... at the Weizmann Institute of Sci...

The First President

Weizmann's homecoming to Eretz Israel was triumphal, in spite of the fact that his country was already called upon, in the moment of its birth, to defend its right to exist, against intransigent Arab armies. Tel Aviv was bombed. Jerusalem was besieged.

Somewhat isolated in Rehovot, where he resided as President-elect, Weizmann was grateful for occasional visits by Jewish commanders. Yigal Allon, in command in the southern sector, wrote that after he had taken Weizmann down to Beersheva to inspect the troops, Weizmann said to him: "This is the first time I have had the feeling of being royalty".

Weizmann had the love, affection and respect of his people, in their land, in whose redemption he had played so big a part. He also was the recipient of tributes from the representatives of the nations.

Israeli and Presidential flags flutter above Weizmann House in Rehovot

Arrival in Israel by Palestine Airways

Settlers welcome their President

Weizmann inspects a guard
of honour in Beer Sheva, escorted by
Yigal Allon and Haim Bar-Lev

Rest — and graffiti —
for a Jerusalem defender

The war in the Galilee

On the road to Gaza

Sprinzak announces the election of Chaim Weizmann as First President of Israel, February 1949

The First President casting the first vote for Israel's first Knesset

Liberated Beer Sheva
welcomes the Weizmanns

The siege lifted, Weizmann enters Jerusalem
with Dov Joseph and Moshe Dayan

Weizmann receives the Ambassadors
of the U.S.S.R. and the U.S.A.

On the occasion of his seventy-fifth birthday, at a banquet in London, General Smuts, the principal speaker, said: "We thank Israel for having reminded us of that last, that only way to salvation (the spiritual force as the answer to the machine)... and especially do we thank Chaim Weizmann for his great leadership and inspiration to the world looking for leadership and inspiration... I love to think of that boy from the Russian ghetto rising to his destiny among the great men of his time... let the Weizmann Forest be the memorial of the great planter, who replanted his people in their ancient homeland... This unique little people, which bequeathed mankind the noblest spiritual heritage of all history, produced also some great, historic leaders of men, foremost among them Moses,

Honouring Weizmann's 75th birthday in London, November 1949,
(l. to r.) Sigmund Gestetner, Viscount Samuel Lord Nathan,
and Field-Marshal Smuts

Sculpture (bronze) by Jacob Epstein,
against a background of an Israeli
fabric design.

the mysterious Founder who first led them out of bondage to this Promised Land, David, the shepherd king, the warrior, the musician and poet, the sinner beloved of God, the conqueror of Jerusalem which he also made the capital of the country. To this historic list, we now add our own contemporary, Chaim Weizmann, the scientist, the great Zionist, the indomitable leader who, after his people had been all but wiped out in the greatest purge of history, assembled the remnants, led them back to the homeland in the face of the heaviest opposition and welded them once more into a sovereign State among the nations".

Celebrating the President's 75th birthday in New York,
(l. to r.) Jasha Heifetz, Dr. Herbert V. Evatt, Australian Foreign Minister,
Mrs Weizmann, Henry Morgenthau, Dewey D. Stone,
Edmund I. Kaufman, Leonard Bernstein and Benjamin Weizmann

243

Torah Scroll presented
by President Weizmann
to President Truman

Haifa greets an immigrant ship

The President at home

Ben-Zvi (who became second President of Israel) and wife Rachel greet President Weizmann while Sharett (Shertok) looks on

The President with his only grandchild,
David Weizmann

Laid to rest

A Prime Minister pays his last respects —
David Ben Gurion and Speaker of the Knesset Joseph Sprinzak

Epilogue
Barnet Litvinoff

Few men are summoned by providence to personify an age. Chaim Weizmann was among them. He was blessed with a vision of the Jewish destiny that could draw upon the memory of countless epochs and yet apply their lessons to a world which changed from day to day. He was a mystic schooled in the disciplines of modern science. His voice had the humility of a pauper, and the majesty of a prophet. His life's achievement was the transformation of a people. The Jews were a suffering race, but no people could be wholly unfortunate if they had a servant like Weizmann.

He was cradled in the Russian ghetto, and his childhood heroes were Moses Montefiore and Edmond de Rothschild. By the time Weizmann was ten years of age the two Jewish princes had initiated a new era in Palestine, and their names were uttered in reverence in the boy's home. Weizmann's later writings tell of the richness of a Jewish family life in the Pale of Settlement when it was presided over by a *Maskil*. Ozer Weizmann was a true child of the Enlightenment, and Motol, the village in White Russia where Chaim was born one hundred years ago, the third of his 11 surviving children, was close enough to Pinsk for exposure to all the new ideas blowing through that hitherto closed world. The father was in the timber trade, not prosperous but certainly outside the pauperised morass in which the bulk of Russian Jewry lived under the Tzars. He ensured that all his children learnt Russian in addition to Hebrew (Yiddish of course was the language of the home) so that they might gain a secular education and enter University. Some 20 years separated the eldest from the youngest, and girls and boys alike were sent out into the world equipped for a profession.

Chaim had chosen chemistry as his life's work. This brought him in young manhood to Berlin and association with student groups largely comprising Russian-Jewish émigrés like himself, and motivated by the same sentiments regarding the need to change the Jewish condition. They drew their inspiration from the Hebrew writer Ahad Ha'am, of Odessa, who taught that the return to their ancestral homeland must be preceded by a spiritual regeneration of the people. In Germany, Weizmann and his friends, among them Leo Motzkin, Shmarya Levin, Joseph Klausner, Martin Buber, Berthold Feiwel and Victor Jacobson, constituted a little army waiting only for a commander. Theodor Herzl was still almost unknown, and political Zionism had still not arrived. But when the Viennese writer summoned his Congress to Basle in 1897 they responded en masse.

They saw in the Zionist Congress, which in the early years met annually, a vehicle for bringing their views to a wider world. Here they could express impatience, criticism, even heresies. They revered their leader but suspected a certain condescension in the sophisticated Herzl towards Russian Jews. Their affinities were more with Menahem Ussishkin, head of the *Hibbat Zion* movement founded in Russia well before Herzl came on the scene.

At the age of 25 Weizmann obtained his doctorate and won a modest teaching post at the University of Geneva. He was soon to make a name in the field of dye-stuffs, registering his first patent in 1902. Later he moved successfully to other branches of chemistry, notably microbiology and the application of fermentation processes. Though from time to time he was compelled to neglect his work in favour of Zionist activities, science was to be his passport to leading academic circles in Europe, then to great industrial concerns, and finally to the world's statesmen.

The young Zionists resented Herzl's

somewhat autocratic conduct of the movement's affairs. Justifiably, they considered that he had little appreciation of the role Jewish culture must play in the national renaissance. He went in search of the political master-stroke that would give them Palestine; they believed with Ussishkin in practical work, both in the land itself and in the Diaspora. Even under Ottoman rule much could be achieved in Palestine, particularly if Zionism became a greater force among the Jews as a whole.

Weizmann saw that their best means of achieving a significant role in Zionism was to address their views through a specific group made up of his generation. He took the leading part in establishing the Democratic Fraction. This was at a Youth Conference that preceded the Fifth Zionist Congress at Basle in 1901. Thus they entered the meeting hall as a bloc of 37 delegates and dominated the proceedings. The first separate party in Zionism was born. Weizmann was recognised as its principal spokesman, a voice from the ranks to be reckoned with in the inner councils of the movement.

Cultural activities were to loom largest in the Democratic Fraction's programme. The campaign turned on an ambitious scheme to create a Jewish University, located either in Europe or Palestine. Weizmann established a bureau in his Geneva lodgings, plunged into organizational work, undertook fund-raising expeditions and propaganda forays. But he was not able to consolidate his early success, and at the end of a year he found himself virtually a voice alone. The students were by definition impermanently established, preoccupied with training for a livelihood, disorganized.

The movement was not then enthusiastic about a University, and in 1903 was urgently concerned with the pogrom in Kishinev that Easter, and an offer by the British Government to grant the Jews a concession for settlement in East Africa. This historic gesture, the first approach of any government to Zionism, was heatedly debated at the Sixth Congress, but the sounds emanating from the Democratic Fraction were barely audible.

The 'Uganda Scheme' as it was termed (though the area was more exactly in Kenya) produced that famous rift between 'politicals' and 'practicals' in the movement which demonstrated that those who felt deepest about the Jewish spiritual revival felt deepest about Palestine. There could be no other place, they said, not even, in Max Nordau's description, for a *Nachtasyl*. Weizmann could not but be among them. Ussishkin rose as the 'practicals' leader, and began to chastise Herzl, now a very sick man, at every turn. Herzl's death, in July 1904, delivered a traumatic blow to the cause but did not still the polemic. A decade of intense controversy ensued, even after 'Uganda' ceased to be an issue.

It was also a watershed for Chaim Weizmann. He had found romance in Geneva, and was due to be married to a medical student there, Vera Khatzman of Rostov-on-Don. It was his moment to break with the student milieu and make more determined advances in his professional career. The future pointed to England, and that same summer he found himself the lonely occupant of a basement laboratory at the University of Manchester, in the department of Prof. William Perkin. A hush momentarily came into his normally gregarious and loquacious way of life as Weizmann busied himself in research.

He was able to supplement his University stipend through part-time employment in the aniline works of Charles Dreyfus, who was both a prominent figure in English Zionism and a leading light of the Manchester Conservative Party. During this early period in England, Weizmann frequently turned for advice to Moses Gaster, a pioneer adherent of Zionism and *Haham* (principal Sephardi rabbi) in England.

Dreyfus and Gaster at once recognised the newcomer as an important recruit to Zionist strength in their country, and as a rising personality in a movement crippled by the premature loss of its founder and bitterly divided as to its next move. One step now followed another in a way Weizmann could never have dreamed possible. Invitations poured in for him to address meetings. In January, 1906, he made the most important political contact of his life with his encounter with Arthur J. Balfour, the ex-Prime Minister, that is so vividly described in his Memoirs, *Trial and Error*. His marriage also took place that year, and in 1907 he delivered his first major address to a Zionist Congress. It was a plea for 'synthetic' Zionism in the hope (mistaken, as it transpired) to unite the differing trends in the movement. Soon afterwards he was on his way for his first visit to the country which had not for a single day been remote from his thoughts since childhood.

The trip was a great educational experience. For some three weeks he travelled north to Beyrout, south to Jaffa, saw Jerusalem, visited the new colonies of Jewish pioneers. He renewed acquaintance with friends of his student days, gained his first glimpse of the Arab world. What he saw confirmed to him that the line the 'practicals' were taking in Zionism was the correct one: within the limitations imposed by Turkish rule, and despite the difficulties placed in the way of immigration, it was still possible to do a great deal in the country. Jews could buy land in small plots, settle people on it, try out pilot plants for future industry. Only ten per cent of the 800,000 population was Jewish. They were mainly old-established residents of low economic and cultural status, and with little hope for their children's future except a life-time of poverty, or emigration.

The 'politicals' who still cast the movement in the Herzlian mould were therefore an incubus. How could he change this? Weizmann had supporters in Manchester, but they were no challenge to the forces in London clinging to the old Zionism, and even England as a whole was dwarfed by the organization's strength on the Continent. However, there was one forum in which Weizmann was influential: at the Zionist Congress he was regularly seated on the Steering Committee, and latterly was elected its Chairman. He used this important behind-the-scenes office to get the movement onto 'practical' rails — a protracted task that took toll of his health and made him not a few enemies, but was in the end successful.

The 'revolution' was achieved at the Tenth Congress, in 1911. Headquarters were transferred from Vienna to Berlin. A new Executive, led by the botanist Otto Warburg, who had long advocated methodical research into Palestine's economic potential, was formed. It contained Weizmann's old comrades Shmarya Levin and Victor Jacobson, as well as the Hebrew writer and scholar Nahum Sokolow. And although Weizmann did not join the Executive himself — it would have involved surrendering his Manchester post and moving to Berlin — they looked to him as an equal.

Meanwhile, what was happening in his personal life? He regularly spent part of his University vacation studying microbiology at the Pasteur Institute in Paris. His work in fermentation was being rewarded with successive patents. He had every hope of a Chair at Manchester, and he was the acknowledged leader of a younger group of English Zionists, among them Harry Sacher, journalist of distinction, and Leon Simon, brilliant Classics scholar and Hebraist.

As we picture the future leader of Jewry in those tranquil times before the First World War, walking his beautiful wife and young son in genteel Welsh holiday resorts, or boarding the tram-car for the half-hour journey down to Cheetham, Manchester's Jewish quarter and location of the Zionist office, or joining local society at a Vice-Chancellor's sherry party, there seemed little wrong with Weizmann's world. But beneath that exterior there stirred a soul that ached for his people suffering humiliating poverty and repeated pogroms in Tzarist Russia. Here, in the England he admired, he himself felt the eternal foreigner — preferred it that way in fact, because the urge to be wholly Jewish was not to be suppressed.

He yearned to live and work in Palestine. A hope arose with the plan to establish the Haifa Technion, an enterprise with which Ahad Ha'am, now resident in London and an intimate friend, was closely associated. But there was no money for a chemistry department, and the project engendered bitter controversy as to the place the Hebrew language would occupy there. Weizmann's spirit was at low ebb when, in 1913, he was passed over in the succession to Perkin's Chair at Manchester.

However, a new, golden vision appeared on the horizon: the Hebrew University, in Jerusalem! This time the auguries were good, and Weizmann readily accepted the invitation to take up his slumbering Geneva project again. It was realistic now because old Baron de Rothschild had intimated his willingness to contribute. The questions were: how much, how soon, under what conditions? The challenge galvanised Weizmann afresh. He brought the difficult negotiations with the Baron to the point of fruition, and began to concern himself with the detailed planning just as the Continent erupted in conflagration.

August, 1914, confronted the Zionists with a cruel dilemma. Jews were not Jews alone. Some were Germans dedicated to their country's victory. Large numbers of Russian Jews, whether serving in the Tzar's armies, or recently arrived in the West, or making a new life in neutral America, detested their native land and prayed for its defeat — as indeed Weizmann had during the Russo–Japanese War of 1905. He was now a British subject owing his loyalty to the ally of hated Russia. What therefore would happen to a movement which transcended national frontiers and whose members stood on either side of the firing lines? With headquarters in Berlin, it had attracted charges of pro-German orientation even before the war. The Executive at that time comprised German and Russian nationals. Manifestly, it could not work as before, and it was arguable whether it could work at all.

Weizmann was a mere Vice-President of the still insignificant English Zionist Federation. Yet he was conscious of being the only European-bred Zionist of importance within a country whose victory would carry enormous influence in the world. He now counted in his following, besides some rising Anglo-Jewish intellectuals, two young Manchester merchants, Simon Marks and Israel Sieff, who had demonstrated eagerness to give generously of their talent and fortune to the cause.

Beyond Zionism, his academic life had brought him friendship with such prominent figures as Arthur Schuster, the physicist, and Samuel Alexander, the philosopher. A casual meeting arising from his wife's medical work was soon to introduce him to C. P. Scott, *Manchester Guardian* Editor and leading Liberal personality. He was known to Balfour and Churchill and to other politicians, Herbert Samuel among them. He was soon to meet Lloyd George. Weizmann's horizons had widened. He was ready for his moment.

This came in November, 1914, with Britain's declaration of war against Turkey. So the future status of Palestine was thrown into the melting-pot, together with all the other Eastern possessions of the Sultan. Many world statesmen knew nothing of modern Zionism, but all knew of the ancient Jewish connection with the Holy Land. Jews the world over were now to matter to both sides in the conflict, particularly in America. Everyone began to woo them. But they also wooed the Arabs. The multi-pathed progress towards the Balfour Declaration had begun.

Weizmann, in common with other leading scientists, was invited in 1915 to employ his knowledge for the war effort. He was appointed a chemical adviser to the Admiralty and the Ministry of Munitions, to work in London. His assignment was to find, from domestic resources, a production method for acetone, required for the manufacture of smokeless gunpowder. The German blockade had led to a grave shortage of the compound, to imperil Britain's firing capacity. Lloyd George was at Munitions, and Churchill at the Admiralty, when Weizmann initiated his work. Soon Lloyd George succeeded as Prime Minister and therefore knew him not only as a Zionist propagandist but also as a man making a vital contribution to Britain's defence.

Further afield, Sokolow was achieving understanding for the cause in journeys between England, France and Italy. Shmarya Levin was in the U.S.A. developing Zionist sentiment among the masses while Justice Louis D. Brandeis was similarly occupied in the upper reaches of authority, beginning with President Wilson, and would soon discuss the subject in Washington with Balfour, now Foreign Secretary. Joseph Trumpeldor had led his Zion Mule Corps on the Gallipoli peninsula.

Thus Weizmann was by no means the lone advocate of the cause. But he occupied the key position, and early in 1917 the English Zionist Federation recognised this by persuading Joseph Cowen to cede the Presidency to him. It was enough. The ex-Russian chemist now assumed the major role in all negotiations. The British, always suspicious of flamboyance, appreciated his quiet method. He spoke, it seemed to them, in the language of the Prophets.

Manifestly, he could not have obtained the Balfour Declaration single handed, and took pains to demolish some such myth throughout his life. The Near East loomed too large in military and political strategy, with too many factors beyond the control of the British, to have occasioned an act of policy of such magnitude on the basis of a single individual's efforts. The activities of Samuel were of immense importance, while Gaster was effective behind the scenes. The Rabbi was a personal friend of Samuel and knew of the latter's Zionist convictions when Weizmann was labelling him an 'Anglo' pure and simple. It was to Gaster that Mark Sykes of the British Cabinet Office, and François Georges-Picot, his French counterpart, turned for information on Zionism while Anglo-French discussions were proceeding on the future of the area. Aaron Aaronson had organized the pro-Ally 'Nili' spy network behind Turkish lines, and Vladimir Jabotinsky, stormy petrel of Zionism, was knocking on Whitehall doors with his plea for a Jewish military formation to join in the liberation of Palestine. Lord Rothschild and other members of his family were demonstrating that Zionism was by no means anathema to all influential circles of the Anglo-Jewish establishment.

Weizmann, however, held all the strands together. He had an instinct for what was and what was not attainable. By the middle of April, 1917, when America entered the war, he had the absolute trust of the Foreign Secretary. Thus the Balfour Declaration of November 2, 1917, pledging His Majesty's Government to 'use their best endeavours for the establishment in Palestine of a national home for the Jewish people' was addressed to the English Zionist Federation. From that moment, the name on all lips was Chaim Weizmann. No Jew in modern times enjoyed such authority and prestige, for the people were at the summit of their expectations.

Weizmann arrived in conquered Jerusalem in April 1918 at the head of a Zionist Commission to begin the rehabilitation of the Jewish community and initiate a programme for the 'national home.' He was met by a host of problems and a chorus of complaints. Wretchedness and hunger induced by the Turkish retreat had brought conflicts, prostitution and social collapse. The Jewish battalions of the Royal Fusiliers, Jabotinsky's achievement, had been kept virtually inactive by G.H.Q. and protested against being left to kick their heels in Egypt. The British, in the main resentful of the Balfour Declaration, discouraged the Commission's attempts to assume the Jew's communal responsibilities. There were refugees in Egypt impatient for repatriation, and the beginnings of discontent among sections of the Arab population.

Weizmann and his colleagues, who included Leon Simon, Israel Sieff, James de Rothschild (Edmond's son, there to represent his father's widespread interests) and Joseph Cowen, with Major William Ormsby-Gore the sympathetic British liaison officer, had to deal with every petty squabble and still retain the vision of an historic endeavour in process of realisation. Weizmann

determined on at least one public demonstration of Zionism's spiritual significance: he insisted, while the guns were still firing, on dedicating the site on Mount Scopus in Jerusalem where the Hebrew University would rise. He told the gathering, which included Arab and Jewish dignitaries in addition to General Allenby, commanding the entire British force in this theatre:

> It seems at first sight paradoxical that in a land with so sparse a population, in a land where everything still remains to be done, in a land crying out for such simple things as ploughs, roads and harbours, we should begin by creating a centre of spiritual and intellectual development. But it is no paradox for those who know the soul of the Jew. It is true that great social and political problems still face us and will demand their solution from us. We Jews know that when the mind is given fullest play, when we have a centre for the development of Jewish consciousness, then coincidentally we shall attain the fulfillment of our material needs.

The words echoed a feeling that the providential alliance between the Jews and what, even after the calamitous war, was still the world's greatest Power would now at last produce the great happening of Messianic dreams — and they were not the dreams of Jews alone — in the rebuilding of the Holy Land as a Jewish State. Weizmann himself would not utter that 'Ineffable Name.' Unlike many Zionists, he knew they were only at the beginning of the road. Important steps still remained before the Balfour Declaration itself would be recognised in international law. Weizmann would have to argue his people's cause again and again, ever resisting pressures from within Zionism as well as outside, and from Jews and non-Jews alike.

First he had to face the Council of Ten at Versailles, in order to place the case for the Jewish right to the Return before the Peace Conference. Next he had to win the endorsement of the San Remo Conference in April 1920, and have the Balfour Declaration incorporated in the Peace Treaty with Turkey, and witness the award to Britain of the Palestine Mandate as a trust on behalf of the League of Nations. It involved discussions with Arab leaders, principally the Hashemite prince Feisal, and allaying their suspicions. Zionism did not visualise the displacement of a single Arab, he assured them, nor limitations upon their own rights of autonomy. He had to accept long, anxious attendance in the ante-rooms of power, but it all seemed to work out right in the end, particularly when Lloyd George invited Herbert Samuel to become the first High Commissioner, and Weizmann was himself elected President of the World Zionist Organization.

Post-war Zionism turned a fresh page in the story of the Jewish people. Russian Jewry had all but ceased to exist as an organized, articulate community, and the Bolsheviks classed Zionism as bourgeois and counter-revolutionary. Millions of others in Eastern Europe were the proscribed subjects of antisemitic regimes in Poland, Hungary and Rumania, and Zionism was their only hope. From London Weizmann issued a call for a great fund-raising operation to help transform much of this *Lumpenproletariat* into pioneers of agriculture and industry in the new Palestine. Arab hostility could not be ignored, but there was evidence also of Arab friendship. The financial problem turned the leader's thoughts to America, where Brandeis reigned supreme. The great jurist did not share Weizmann's traditional loyalties to the movement. He was prepared to scrap the entire machine, leave relief to the philanthropists and economic development to investment experts. A clash was unavoidable.

Weizmann's victory over Brandeis took place at Cleveland, Ohio, in June, 1921. A new Zionist Organization of America was forged. It was led by Louis Lipsky, of Rochester, New York, a man of literary proclivities who brought with him, among others, a young Polish immigrant, Meyer Weisgal. Together these two fostered the Weizmann cause in America in the way that Marks, Sieff and Sacher, all brothers-in-law now and at the head of the Marks and Spencer department store chain, were doing in England. The result was that every succeeding visit of Weizmann to America became a triumph. He came to inspire, to solve complicated problems of organization, to enroll talent as well as funds.

Of hardly less significance for the future was America's recognition of Weizmann as a chemist of genius. He had shown during the war that fermentation could be turned to large-scale industrial application. He taught that the globe contained great natural resources lying fallow, and could be used not merely in times of war but in the general raising of living standards. He was not of course the only scientist to come to this conclusion, but he was ahead of most in the field, with processes ready for which there were immediate purchasers in America. His income therefrom and from the award given him by the British government for his war-time acetone work, added strength to his Jewish leadership, in that he was not a Zionist 'doing it for a living.'

More battles were to come. Throughout the twenties and early thirties, Weizmann was virtually under constant attack. Many of his followers interpreted his faith in Britain as weakness. They accused him of accepting too readily a progressive contraction of the true meaning of the Balfour

Declaration. As one Congress followed another his reports grew more troubled, and he felt betrayed. His reproaches were divided equally between the Jews, who expected too much from others, too little from themselves, and the British, who confronted the ever-growing militancy of the Arabs under their leader Haj Amin el Husseini, Mufti of Jerusalem, with ambiguity and hesitation. Palestine had an economic slump in 1927, and more Jews left the country than arrived — despite the distressed condition of East European Jewry, which became the Zionist prize for the rival electioneering endeavours of David Ben-Gurion as workers' champion and Jabotinsky and his right-wing Revisionists. The latter had the support of *Mizrachi,* the religious Zionists who had never been enthusiastic for Weizmann.

As a figure above party, Weizmann did not enjoy the support of an organized machine, and there was a grass-roots rebellion against his style of leadership when he faced the 1931 Congress at Basle and a call that he make a forthright demand for a Jewish State. Of course he too wanted this, but, he replied, 'my belief in the justice of our cause, and a grave sense of responsibility, do not permit me to indulge in fantasies, or to suggest adventurous policies which can only lead to heartbreaking disappointments. Instead of chasing a mirage, and wasting our efforts in futile internecine strife over shadows, let us concentrate on what is within reach of a reasonable possibility — first of all on the consolidation of the work that has already begun in Palestine.'

They would not have it. The Congress refused to re-elect him President. Who would succeed him? Some thought it must be Jabotinsky, the exponent of maximalism. But the choice went, ironically, to Sokolow, the man always identified with Weizmann's

policy and who had collaborated loyally with him. In disowning their only leader of world stature they had rejected one moderate for another.

A retrospective view shows that Weizmann's freedom from day-to-day tasks was not altogether a misfortune. He could now address himself to longer-term problems. He gave attention to the Hebrew University, warned against the increasing urbanisation of the *Yishuv,* and the growth of a 'peddlar class' that reminded him of the ghettos of the East. When Hitler came to power in 1933, giving heightened urgency to the demand for relaxing Palestine's immigration controls against the Jews, he became absorbed particularly in recruiting people of his talent. Here was a tragic irony indeed! German-Jewish intellectuals such as Einstein were leaving their adored *Vaterland* to escape persecution; a Jewish land hungered to embrace and honour them. Yet they seemed to prefer to go almost anywhere than to Palestine.

He intended spending six months each year at the Hebrew University, for he felt he had too long neglected his greatest love, pure research. Astonishingly, he was refused a laboratory there, on financial grounds. But the true reason was that the University Head, Judah Magnes, resented Weizmann's criticism of his academic policy. Thus the Chairman of Governors was denied a base in the institution he had virtually founded!

Well, why concentrate everything in Jerusalem? He recalled his 1907 visit to Rehovot, a settlement then in the midst of desert, with a striking view of Ramleh from its hill-crest. It contained a small agricultural research station. In 1933 Weizmann's close English friends Israel and Rebecca Sieff lost a 17 year-old son in tragic circumstances. A memorial that would serve humanity might solace them. This took the historic form of the Daniel

Sieff Research Institute, established in 1934 through the generosity of the Marks-Sieff-Sacher family — 'the Family' as it was known. Weizmann sent out a call to German-Jewish scientists, no longer honoured in their homeland, to join him there. Some refused him. But his recruits did include, among others, the brothers David and Felix Bergmann, who were destined to be of great service to Israel in peace and war. They made important discoveries in the reactions of various anhydrides, and conducted research into the preparation of proteins and pharmaceuticals.

David Bergmann became Weizmann's scientific *alter ego,* shouldering the entire burden of establishing the Sieff Institute. Proud though he was of their work there, Weizmann sought to discourage the popular lore that grew from reports by visitors who loved Zionism more than they understood science. It embarrassed him. 'Make molehills out of mountains, not the reverse,' he once begged Weisgal. Nevertheless out of the Rehovot establishment there germinated one of the great research institutions of our day: the Weizmann Institute of Science.

Meanwhile, the Sokolow interregnum was serving only to illustrate that Weizmann's leadership was more than ever essential to the movement, and the demand for his return grew to a clamour. Immigration into Palestine was still at a low ebb in 1931, but the signs were that under the impact of Hitlerism a huge swell of newcomers would reach the country. It was to the credit of the government that, despite strong displeasure from the Arabs, 130,000 were allowed in between 1933–35. Still, the number of immigration permits issued was totally inadequate for the demand, and the process of organized 'illegal' entry was born.

Amid scenes of tremendous enthusiasm, and sighs of general relief, Weizmann resumed his place as leader at the Zionist Congress in Lucerne, 1935. They now recognised him for what he was: a severe critic among themselves, a fearless advocate when confronting the British. Prior to the Congress he had spoken out in Palestine against the decline of the spirit of pioneering, and land-speculation. What, he demanded angrily, had happened to their respect for natural beauty, their love of simplicity? The formula for Weizmann's return had been the work of Ben-Gurion: he himself would be the Chairman of the Jewish Agency Executive, Weizmann its President. Ussishkin, long scornful of Weizmann's policy of gradualism, was delighted. Stephen Wise, who had led his American delegation into the opposition in 1931, termed the Lucerne Congress his 'Sabbath of Repentance.' The Arabs watched and waited.

Ben-Gurion's accession to high office reflected the new realities in Zionism. The *Yishuv* had grown to nearly 400,000, and though the Arabs had likewise increased, the Jews were now 30 per cent of the whole. By virtue of its superior organization and the pioneering will of its best elements, the Zionist Left predominated in the country. The branches of Ben-Gurion's power extended from its trade union trunk to industrial activities, political work, communal villages. He was involved in clandestine Jewish self-defence preparations, and kept in touch with international socialist bodies. Now he was also second-in-command of the Zionist movement. Weizmann was not a Marxist, but he welcomed Ben-Gurion because he recognised that the most self-less Zionism and the most difficult toil belonged to the workers' movement. But there would be profound differences. Ben-Gurion had emerged from the rough and tumble of internal Palestine politics, Weizmann was a product of the

Zionist Congress, with a positive attitude to the Diaspora. Ben-Gurion believed that in the final reckoning between Jews, British and Arabs, the strength of the *Yishuv* would be the decisive factor; his Chief employed his unparalleled authority with statesmen everywhere to avoid such a reckoning.

The Arabs observed that the world that had endorsed the Balfour Declaration was clearly coming to an end. Their own national movement was now on the march, and it served notice that the undisputed power of Britain and France was not in the permanent order of things, in the Middle East or elsewhere. Japan had invaded Manchuria, Mussolini Ethiopia, and Germany had just defied the League of Nations by entering the Rhineland. Evidently force paid. But the dynamic of Jewish progress warned the Mufti of Jerusalem that the morrow might be too late. He moved in April, 1936. An Arab Higher Committee was established in Nablus, and a general strike declared to compel the stoppage of Jewish immigration and land sales, and the creation of an Arab government. This marked the end of co-existence in Palestine. The difference between Weizmann and Ben-Gurion now became the difference between the pen and the sword.

As we have seen, Weizmann's immense strength lay in his personal capacities. His whisper was more potent than a hundred demonstrations. This gave rise to the charge that his diplomacy was too private (the charge Weizmann had once himself levelled against Herzl), that he acted without consultation. But Zionism had no quasi-government in permanent session in any one place. Executive members sat both in Jerusalem and London, and were largely interchangeable. Weizmann worked mainly from Great Russell Street, their Bloomsbury headquarters, and there the Executive included, over sustained periods, Berl

Locker and Moshe Shertok (later Sharett) of the Left, and Selig Brodetsky and Nahum Goldmann of the Centre, besides Ben-Gurion himself. Weizmann would not move without clearing matters of substance with them. He had other advisers — they were more than Civil Servants, less than policy-makers: Arthur Lourie, Cambridge-trained lawyer, Lewis Namier the historian, and Balfour's niece, Blanche ('Baffy') Dugdale. They drafted memoranda, advised on Weizmann's speeches, dug out research, smoothed over difficult moments with Ben-Gurion. Together they constituted what they termed the *Yeshivah,* and hammered out problems among themselves to produce recommendations for the President on a possible course of action. Weizmann developed relations of deep affection with Shertok, whom he trusted to support his line in Palestine, and with Locker, humanist and Yiddish wit. Baffy Dugdale was in a category by herself, related as she was to a large part of the Anglo-Scottish aristocracy. Confidante of members of the Conservative Cabinet, this gentile Zionist was beloved by all and on occasion presided at meetings of the *Yeshivah.*

Arab guerillas infiltrated Palestine with the strike, but the government temporised and the Jews chose to reply with a policy of *Havlagah,* 'self-restraint.' But they consolidated their position by developing *Haganah* and occupying the economic hiatus created by the Arab stoppage. The British garrison was enlarged, and enlarged again. A Royal Commission was appointed under Lord Peel, by no means the last but the one Weizmann was to describe as 'the ablest of the investigating bodies ever sent out to Palestine.'

Against a gathering crescendo of Arab terrorism, with the mining of roads and railways, murder in the streets, and the intimidation of Arab moderates by the

Mufti's followers, the Peel Commission dismissed Arab grievances as largely unfounded, pointing to their economic and social progress due to the Zionist presence, and their rapidly increasing population in Palestine. Nevertheless the aspirations of the two communities were incompatible. Peel therefore recommended the division of the country into Jewish and Arab States, with a large chunk, including Jerusalem, to remain as British mandated territory. So the 'Ineffable Name' had been uttered: a Jewish State. And by Britain herself!

It was only a morsel, the north-western tip of Palestine, one-fifth of its area this side of the Jordan. Yet both Weizmann and Ben-Gurion saw the possibilities. United, they faced a difficult Congress in 1937, imploring delegates to keep the door open. It was the closest the two were to come, and they managed to carry the Congress with them. Then, the great betrayal. As the world slipped towards the disaster of the Second World War, and the Western Powers initiated a policy of appeasement, and German persecution drove the Jews to desperation, the government retracted. Malcolm MacDonald, well-meaning Colonial Secretary in the Chamberlain administration, had to bring the news to Weizmann ('I'll never speak to that *shaigitz* again,' commented the Jewish leader bitterly, in contemptuous Yiddish). There followed the organized mockery of the St. James's Conference, with the Arab refusal to sit together with the Jews. The Balfour Declaration dissolved into the 1939 White Paper and the Land Transfer Ordinances. A maximum of 75,000 Jews would be allowed in during the next five years, and subsequently only with the consent of the Arabs. In ten years, Palestine, with its overwhelming Arab majority, would be granted independence. In the meantime the Jews could only buy land, or plant a tree, or put in a water-supply, in one-twentieth of the country's area. It was a Zionist death certificate. Weizmann said: 'The sorrow is ours, the shame is theirs.' Such was the situation at the outbreak of war. Weizmann did speak to that *shaigitz* again, but he now had a really powerful friend in the Cabinet — Winston Churchill.

The democracies' struggle was Jewry's struggle. That was obvious. Weizmann sent a personal letter to Prime Minister Chamberlain pledging all aid, and a truce in Palestine. Ben-Gurion used a famous phrase with a different emphasis: 'We shall fight the war as if there were no White Paper, and the White Paper as if there were no war.' He strove to keep Jewish grievances alive. So did others within Palestine: Jews began to hear of the existence of a body described as the *Irgun*. Weizmann, supported by the Americans under Rabbi Hillel Silver, and the vast body of Zionists, saw activism as an ill-omen for the future. He hoped for a gesture from the government to help him restrain extremism in the *Yishuv*. He hoped in vain.

He was now 65, and had acquired a status in science that numbered him among a select handful of bio-chemists of world renown. He was appointed honorary chemical adviser to the British Ministry of Supply, and in this capacity sent David Bergmann from the Sieff Institute to Paris to work on aromatisation processes for the turning of heavy oils into a range of adaptable by-products. When France fell in June, 1940, Bergmann came to London to pursue his research in Weizmann's laboratory there.

Britain, in Weizmann's eyes, was too complacent about her supplies during the early part of the war. She counted on food and *matériel* from America, oil from the Middle East, rubber from Malaya. But the blockade could harden, the Arab world did not admit loyalty to the Allies, and distant

Malaya was close to Japan. Yet the almost limitless vegetation of India and Africa, which could be rendered into synthetic products, was being neglected. Moreover, huge quantities of maize and wheat were at the time going to waste in the United States and Canada because shipping shortages prevented their export. He begged friends in the Cabinet, notably Leo Amery, who had played a part in the drafting of the Balfour Declaration, to utilise their chemical properties. He undertook two long visits to the United States to put these proposals to the Baruch Committee in Washington. Bergmann went over as his personal scientific representative.

As it happened, the vested interests of big business in America, particularly the oil companies, helped to block some of Weizmann's most significant recommendations, and his processes were left to commercial exploitation after the war. Such considerations were not so strong at Rehovot. The Sieff Institute went over to the development of pharmaceuticals for the military, though here again the full implementation of his ideas was restricted by a reluctance to provide him with certain essential materials.

Science was a refuge not only from political cares but also his private grief. His younger son Michael, a Cambridge physicist and engineer 26 years old, and R.A.F. flight lieutenant, was in February 1942 lost on a mission over the Bay of Biscay. It was a tragedy from which neither Weizmann nor his wife Vera, who had been doing medical work in the London air-raids, would ever fully recover.

The war was becoming a great test of endurance for the aging leader. A brother and sister were beyond contact somewhere in Russia. Palestine seemed remote, and the home he and Vera had built in Rehovot had been so little used. More than this, the entire Jewish world now looked to him as its patriarch, its family head, and he received endless letters from private individuals seeking his intercession with governments for visas for relatives, or information about their fate in Europe which he could know no better than they. He had to make repeated appeals to officialdom on behalf of refugees carried in ships that had no place to harbour, such as the *Patria* and *Struma,* coffin boats that went down with over a thousand lives lost.

Though discussion of Palestine's constitutional future might be suspended, Weizmann pursued one immediate claim, which was also an offering. This was for a Jewish fighting force to take its place among the Allies under its own colours, as in the case of the expatriate Poles, Czechs, etc. Jews of course served in all the armies of the free world, and large numbers — more in fact than the War Office would accept — were volunteering in Palestine. They were being restricted because of British anxiety to maintain uniformed Arabs at a parity, and the latter enlisted only in the smallest numbers. Churchill was known to be in favour of the force, as were others in the Cabinet. But Anthony Eden, War Minister and later Foreign Secretary, was an Arabophile with plans for the Middle East that took little cognizance of the Jews, and of course the Colonial Office was also obstructive. Prior to his first wartime visit to the U.S.A., a journey undertaken as much for the government as for Zionist purposes, Weizmann let it be known to Churchill that American Jewry, the only community in that country wholly committed to a British victory, would respond most if the Jews of Palestine were accepted for what they were, an enthusiastic ally.

Ben-Gurion felt that Weizmann was not pressing hard enough. He regarded Britain's pleas of equipment shortages as excuses, and demanded public protests. Weizmann thought these would embarrass the government in the prosecution of the war. The two became estranged. Ben-Gurion resented Weizmann's privileged approach to Cabinet members, not accorded to himself. He described the *Yeshivah* meetings at Great Russell Street not as Weizmann taking counsel but as Weizmann 'holding court.' A year went by, and at last Weizmann agreed that they should publicise their complaint against the government. The world was alerted to Britain's failure fully to mobilise Jewish manpower and goodwill, and Palestine's economic potential, in the cause.

Weizmann in America. The adulation with which he was greeted in New York and across the country did not deceive him. He was shocked by the contrast between conditions in war-wounded Europe and the frivolities of a country ascended to a level of prosperity never known before, and which largely saw the war as a localised conflict fed by competing national interests. There was substantial, unexpected support for Germany. Of course the Jews prayed for Hitler's downfall, but nowhere did he observe a reflex of anguish for their people's fate in Poland, Austria, Czechoslovakia (France and the Low Countries had not yet fallen). The parochialism of the rival Zionist groups and their absorption in trivialities filled him with distaste, and, apart from Louis Lipsky and Stephen Wise, no longer young, there were no top calibre leaders.

Directing his attentions to Washington, he had interviews with President Roosevelt, Cordell Hull and other members of the Administration. He established relations with Jewish members of the President's entourage, among them Samuel Rosenman, Henry Morgenthau Jr., Felix Frankfurter, Ben Cohen — though not Bernard Baruch,

who excluded himself from Jewish attachments. In this he had valuable assistance from Israel Sieff, then on an extended visit to Washington.

Weizmann delegated Meyer Weisgal, a man with the imagination to transcend organizational loyalties, to keep his Zionist policies alive in America and mount a national conference in New York embracing all branches of the Zionist movement. It was time, Weizmann now conceded, to let the hitherto uninformed American public know of their frustrations in relations with the Mandatory Power. There were many postponements of the conference, but Weizmann would not let the idea die. It was as though he wished by his efforts alone to bring American Jewry onto the European front. Then came Pearl Harbour, and the work was done for him.

That conference met at the Biltmore Hotel in May, 1942, and heard major policy addresses by Weizmann and Ben-Gurion. It did not have the historical magnitude with which it was credited. It demanded that Palestine become a 'Jewish Commonwealth', a term used by Weizmann some months earlier in an article in the quarterly *Foreign Affairs* without specifying its application to the country as a whole. The Biltmore resolution, Weizmann subsequently admitted, was extravagant. Its main effect was to warn Britain that American Zionism at last had teeth; and the leader now knew that his every action would be scrutinised for signs of weakness.

There was an open rift with Ben-Gurion, who saw that Weizmann was losing ground in America. Ben-Gurion repeated his allegations of lack of consultation and timidity on Weizmann's part. He returned to Palestine, where relations between British and Jews (still unable to get into a 'Jewish' uniform) had reached a sorry pass. The Arabs did not conceal their delight at

Germany's successes in the early phase of the Middle East war, and the Mufti was now operating from Berlin. The Jews replied by hoarding arms in their settlements, and a cadre of permanent Jewish troops, unofficially accepted by the British and used by them in the invasion of Vichy-held Syria, was organized to protect the *Yishuv*.

Back in London, Weizmann's tone towards the government grew sharper. He had won important allies in Washington and knew that his people expected a new toughness from him. News of the Nazi extermination policy against the Jews was now leaking through. The British were conducting arms searches in Palestine with the clumsy brutality usually accompanying such operations.

In the general degeneration of the Palestine situation the *Irgun* had given birth to a violent wing, the Stern Group. Nevertheless Weizmann was making headway in Whitehall, mainly because he could always go over the heads of Cabinet subordinates and get a message through to the Prime Minister. At last, in September 1944, the government announced that a Jewish Brigade would be organized to participate in the liberation of Europe. Two months later Lord Moyne, Minister of State in the Middle East, was assassinated by the Sternists. Churchill felt betrayed.

The momentum of change in war-time Palestine had in fact left Weizmann out of touch with events there. Under Ben-Gurion the *Yishuv* was becoming a national base that saw much of what transpired in Diaspora Zionism as irrelevant. Inside the *Yishuv* opposing forces confronted each other with great bitterness, for Ben-Gurion's writ did not extend to the extremists of *Irgun* and Stern. Weizmann's health, never robust, had broken under his private and public cares. He first complained in July, 1942, of the eye-trouble that would one day bring him to near-blindness, and the following year he was compelled to rest for months at a time. He confessed to thoughts of resignation, principally because the Palestine Executive was presided over by a man 'with whom I find myself in disagreement on essential points,' a man who 'was hurtful to the best interests of the movement, undermined my authority and wasted my time.'

At the end of 1944 a tired Weizmann was able to return home and to his scientific institute in Rehovot. It was as though a king had returned to his subjects after long exile. The messages of welcome poured in from every school in the *Yishuv*, every municipality, every organization, from individuals claiming acquaintance from his Pinsk boyhood, and his student days. As he toured the country the crowds massed for a glimpse of him. Zionist enterprise was evidenced everywhere — in yellow desert turned lush with crops, irrigation pipes whirring, Tel Aviv a sprawling metropolis — all within the straitjacket of the White Paper and land transfer prohibitions. But he was still the old Weizmann, still the severe judge no less than the great defender of his people. He wrote of his anxieties to Felix Frankfurter — about the 'political atomisation', as he called it, of the *Yishuv*, which he ascribed to 'insufficient outlets for a concentrated intelligentsia.' He saw immigration as essential, 'for when it stops energies are diverted to fruitless discussion and political fermentation...People become introspective, isolated, provincial.'

Europe was on the point of liberation. Churchill was being acclaimed as the saviour of civilisation, and Weizmann sent him a case of citrus from his Rehovot plantation, a birthday gift, he said, 'from one septuagenarian to another.' Churchill, having inspired his people throughout the war, came to them in 1945 only to be rejected.

A similar fate now awaited Weizmann.

With the arrival of a Labour government in a much-weakened Britain, Weizmann found himself in negotiation with men who could not grasp the change in Jewish mood caused by the horror of Hitler's extermination policy — a crime of Christendom without parallel in history. During the war Weizmann had found Ernest Bevin, then in Churchill's Cabinet, to be open to persuasion on his scientific ideas and not unsympathetic to Zionism. Now, as Foreign Secretary, Bevin greeted his request for the immediate transfer of 100,000 Jews from the European cemetery to Palestine with hostility. He resented the power of American Jewry and knew that Silver had organized a strong Zionist lobby to get President Truman to reinforce the demand. Bevin would not surrender over the 100,000 even after its recommendation by the Anglo–American Committee of Enquiry in 1946. The response was increased militancy in Palestine and increased immigration of Jews via clandestine routes, with scenes of deportation from Palestine's coastline that outraged world opinion. While Weizmann in London was adamant against armed resistance ('I know where it begins, I don't know where it ends') *Haganah* joined secretly with the *Irgun* to coordinate activities.

He made his stand that December, at the Mustermesse in Basle, where the Congress met in the fiftieth year of political Zionism. The question at issue was whether they should accept the government's invitation to resume discussions in London adjourned the previous September, and what should be their minimum demand. Weizmann, sure he would carry the Congress with him, refused to turn his back on negotiation. But the most strident voice belonged to Silver, who had the bulk of American votes behind him and left Stephen Wise, still faithful to Weizmann, with an isolated group of moderates who included Nahum Goldmann and Selig Brodetsky — one had little following, the other little standing. Talk was free at the Congress of Weizmann's role being reduced, and that instead of dropping the old pilot he should be made their Honorary President. He retorted tartly: 'Thank you very much, but don't give me any *mitzvot* while I am still alive.'

Seventeen sessions of the Congress, and still no decision. It all hinged on an agreement between the Americans and the Left, in fact Silver and Ben-Gurion. Weizmann pleaded that his way was still the only possible path: 'If terror becomes the dominating factor in Jewish life the Agency will not be able to control it; on the other hand it may control the Agency.' And when Silver's shadow, Emmanuel Neumann interrupted the President with the cry 'Demagogue!' Weizmann rounded upon him with a reprimand that has become his testament: 'There is a drop of my blood in every workshop in Tel Aviv, in every barn in Nahalal.' In the course of a 24-hour session Weizmann's policy was still neither endorsed nor rejected, and an Executive had still not been formed. The President left the forum. He told a friend that the Mandatory Power was most guilty for the break. He had always been Britain's staunch defender, yet it left him empty-handed, to fight the battle alone. Just one gesture, for example ending the deportation of 'illegal' immigrants, and moderation might have carried the day.

In the event, the Silver — Ben-Gurion axis produced an Executive minus a President, with responsibility divided between Washington and Jerusalem. Narrowly, the Congress voted not to attend the London Conference. But the leaders talked with Bevin just the same, in a vain quest for a solution based upon partition. It was a solution that Weizmann claimed they could have had two years earlier, from Churchill, but for the assassination of Moyne. The scene shifted to the U.N. General Assembly in New York. But it was not yet the final curtain for Jewry's great statesman.

As this narrative approaches its close we again encounter Weizmann in his role of peerless advocate of the Zionist cause. Palestine was sliding towards anarchy. The final commission of enquiry, UNSCOP, decided that partition it must be, with the termination of the British connection and the internationalisation of Jerusalem. Weizmann then appeared before the U.N. *Ad Hoc* Committee in New York considering this recommendation. The scheme provided for the incorporation of most of the Negev, from the Beersheba sub-district to the Red Sea, within the Jewish area. However, the American State Department would not have this. It felt that Arab objections to a Jewish State would be mollified if the Negev were placed within their territory. The Russians, on the other hand, demanded acceptance of the UNSCOP Report *in toto*.

Campaign headquarters for the Jews was Weizmann's suite at the Waldorf Astoria. Two men alone could defeat the State Department's intention to surrender the Negev: himself, frail now and exhausted, and Truman, in Washington. The latter had by then had enough of Zionists of the Silver brand, but Weizmann's name had not lost its magic. Weizmann was received by the President on November 19, 1947, and was promised the Negev, to include Eilat, with Beersheba going to the Arabs. The United Nations accepted the UNSCOP Report on November 29. Britain undertook to leave Palestine by midnight, May 14, 1948.

Weizmann returned to England to prepare his move to Palestine and be among his people in their hour of triumph. The country was already virtually partitioned, with Ben-Gurion the Jewish Prime Minister in fact if not in name. But the debates were not going well in New York. So violent was the Arab reaction to the U.N. decision that it was feared the Jews would not be able to hold their state. Once again the State Department got to work, to suspend partition and substitute a regime of U.N. Trusteeship.

It will be recalled that 1948 was a Presidential election year, and the auguries were not promising for Truman. The Zionists were not backward in their warnings about the Jewish vote if the State Department got its way. Silver was a declared Republican anyway, and Truman expressed his displeasure with the Zionists' rough-handed tactics by refusing them an audience. Once again thoughts centred on Weizmann. He postponed his journey to Palestine, returned to America and had a meeting with Truman on March 18. The President confirmed that, State Department or no, he would see the Jewish State through. War was already raging in Palestine. But within hours of Ben-Gurion's declaration of Israel's independence, America announced its *de facto* recognition. Two days later Chaim Weizmann was invited to be President of the world's youngest nation.

To many, the translation of the ghetto child from the village of Motol to become the First President of the Jewish Commonwealth re-born after 2,000 years, is a story without a happy ending. Perhaps so. The absence of his name from the Declaration of Independence outrages history. The conduct of Prime Minister Ben-Gurion towards the President in Rehovot during the four years of life still left to him offends the concept of brotherhood. Reasons there are for what transpired: Weizmann's life was given to the Jews as a whole, while the signatories on Israel's Magna Charta owe their place there to party loyalties; the Presidential role in Israel's form of democracy was limited to formalities; Weizmann was old and tired and almost sightless, Ben-Gurion young and immediately preoccupied with his State's survival.

Documents, however, are ephemera, and national panoply a hollow glory. Greatness compels a man to walk alone. It was the spirit of Chaim Weizmann, not his actions, that ennobled Jewry. And while this people live he will be crowned among its immortals.